SAVAGE SOLITUDE

First published in 2013 by
The Dedalus Press
13 Moyclare Road
Baldoyle
Dublin 13
Ireland

www.dedaluspress.com

ISBN 978 1 906614 63 8

Dedalus Press titles are represented in the UK by
Central Books, 99 Wallis Road, London E9 5LN
and in North America by Syracuse University Press, Inc.,
621 Skytop Road, Suite 110, Syracuse, New York 13244.

Cover image: Dead Acacia Tree, Namib Desert, Namibia
© Hein Welman | Dreamstime.com

The Dedalus Press receives financial assistance from
The Arts Council / An Chomhairle Ealaíon

SAVAGE SOLITUDE
Reflections of a Reluctant Loner

Máighréad Medbh

DEDALUS PRESS
DUBLIN, IRELAND

Author's Note

HOW TO BE ALONE is the single salient question of this book. There's no single answer, but is there a method without madness or despair? The question is explored in a series of dramatic dialogues based on experience and research. There are three personae: *One; The Other;* and *I.* Together they constitute an individual self.

One is driven by instinct and emotion, and is the part of self we might experience as our core. It can't be properly expressed in ordinary dialogue, because it won't compromise and doesn't speak aloud.

The Other is an aggregate of wider society. Its voice consists of quotations from philosophers, writers, scientists, poets, theologians, mystics and loners.

I is the synthesising consciousness, and the only voice that listens in order to understand. It could be thought of as the planning faculty of the brain.

Reluctant is a key word. The reluctant loner is burdened both by the state and by resistance to the state. Can the longing for companionship ever be satisfied, or can it, should it, be overcome?

"'All our knowledge comes to this,
That existence is enough,
That in savage solitude
Or the play of love
Every living creature is
Woman, Man, and Child'."
– W. H. Auden

"Since we have decided to live alone, without companionship, let our happiness depend on us and no other; let us sever the ties between ourselves and others, thereby allowing us to live well and truly alone, and to do so at our leisure."
– Michel de Montaigne

Contents

⌒

Part 1: If One is to Live

Part 2: The Dangerous World

Part 3: Perspective

⌒

Appendices

PART 1: IF ONE IS TO LIVE

One

I am a drop
Shed by the gregarious sea.
Why do I mourn?

I am a signal
Shot from the electromagnetic bow.
Why do I shake?

I am a pebble
Smashed from the face of an ancient rock.
Why do I bleed?

I am a grain
Sieved from a silent desert.
Why do I crave?

I am a spark
Pitched from a dying star.
Why do I rage?

I am a spot
Jostled in a pixelated world.
Why do I walk?

I am a pulse
Pushed from the sun's hot heart.
Why do I dance?

I am a gasp
Sent from the throat of a wind.
Why do I sing?

shed by the gregarious sea

1. the darkest hour

One

Moving unobserved between rows of curtained houses, aware of other lives in their intimate confidence. There is no map, no plan. The house One has left is transient and silent as bone. One is the odd number, the shape that does not fit, the traveller beside whom no other walks. One's death would hardly be an event. The world would shrug at its cosy dinner table, carry on laughing at its cryptic jokes. Death would end this pain. But if One is to live, how?

The Other

"Thus each of us had to be content to live only for the day, alone under the vast indifference of the sky. This sense of being abandoned, which might in time have given characters a finer temper, began, however, by sapping them to the point of futility."

– Albert Camus: *The Plague*

I

Whatever has caused you to be veiled, like the victim of some faery prank, you're still conscious of yourself. Each heavy footstep is a real act, each tortured question a real thought. Dare to look around. Seek facts. There's no guarantee that all those others are in a state of buzzing bliss.

2. bird

One
A flock of birds traverses the silent sky. Today, it is the only event that has made impact. For a moment One knows what it is to be borne on the wind, unasking.

The Other
"Only that day dawns to which we are awake."
– Henry David Thoreau: *Walden*

I
Birds fly without thought. I, being human, must think. Alone, I carry thought as a burden. If I were to empty my mind, would I be bird, and is that bliss?

3. soundless

One
All sounds are swept into silence, from the rustling of trees to the garrulous torrent of human media. As though One were surrounded by a field that shocks them into small, sub-aural flakes. There is chattering in here, One's own, but that has no sound either, just tireless insistence, like an ineffable sea.

The Other
"There is always something to see, something to hear. In fact, try as we may to make a silence, we cannot.... Until I die there will be sounds. And they will continue following my death. One need not fear about the future of music."
– John Cage: *Silence: Lectures and Writings by John Cage*

I
Everything vibrates, and vibration is sound. Be honest. It's not sound you lack but human speech, and that with meaning, directed towards you.

4. pathless

One
The limpid silence is a land without carp, censure or discernible danger. Neither crop nor creature inhabits; there is no haven or prison. The terrain is pathless. One looks to the sky, waiting for the pole star to rise, but it is not that world.

The Other
"A human being is spirit. But what is spirit? Spirit is the self. But what is the self? The self is a relation that relates itself to itself or is the relation's relating itself to itself in the relation; the self is not the relation but is the relation's relating to itself. A human being is a synthesis of the infinite and the finite, of the temporal and the eternal, of freedom and necessity, in short, a synthesis. A synthesis is a relation between two. Considered in this way, a human being is still not a self."

– Søren Kierkegaard: *The Sickness unto Death*

I
I'm fired up by relevance, created by context. A single point in a dark universe might as well not exist. Even two points are without context. Create a triangle and there's pattern— the force that drives the mind. In the brain, the map is the same as the territory. I must begin to draw.

5. microcosm

One

Acutely aware of constituent parts. Stomach churns, fingers tighten, anus twitches. Tongue snakes around teeth, testing for imperfections. Obsessed with each potentially noxious smell. Examining the hands, poking the nose, listening to each ache and rumble as though they were phone calls. It is an engaging world in here.

The Other

"Retire into your own little territory. That's not only allowed, it's necessary."
– Marcus Aurelius: *Meditations*

I

Obsession with the body is common among loners, probably springing from a primal fear of contamination. You're a child whose attention I must manage, and whose behaviour is a constant worry.

6. pedestrian

One

Hitch-hiker of the psyche. To own a vehicle seems as likely as flying to Venus. One lapses into daydream to the accompaniment of word-swish and commerce, detests Oneself. The others are purposed, moving in coherent directions.

The Other

"The solo expedition, travelling beyond reach, is a big thing and will always be. To the loner, such an adventure promises epiphanies, wonders never to be forgotten, elemental challenges, confrontations with the ultimate and the self. Success or death. The very essence of a loner's life, larger than life."

– Anneli Rufus: *Party of One*

I

This lone odyssey, undertaken with courage, might be sufficient in itself, though it's a switchback trek from oblivion to oblivion. I'm not convinced.

7. singular

One
Where is the *Yes*, the echo of self? Nothing, no other, is quite like. One sends out feelers, reaches only the reaching.

The Other
"... the flowering of life depends upon finding a reflection of oneself in the world."
– Thomas Moore: *The Care of the Soul*

I
That you have no twin might be nature's imprimatur. Is it sameness you seek, and not individuality?

8. chimeras

One
As though waking from a long sleep. It is clear how different
One is and it makes One ashamed. Have longed for a lover.
Invented one in imaginings, also friends. They came, but
could not be held. After a time they all became incompre-
hensible or intrusive. Now heavy in the memory their hurt,
incredulous faces, their accusations. *You*, they say. *Who?* The
nebulous but deadly. One.

The Other
"The impossibility of grasping realities threw me into the
land of chimeras, and, seeing nothing in existence which was
worthy of my enthusiasm, I sought nourishment for it in an
ideal world, which my fertile imagination soon peopled with
beings after my own heart."
– Jean-Jacques Rousseau: *The Confessions*

I
Inner and outer realities are blinkered racers who neither
see each other nor converse. A fantasy friend is a puppet; a
real one lifts his arm without warning, curdles her lip, re-
orders your perspective. If you can't tolerate, it's best that
you stay apart. Disapproval is not for sharing.

9. on the dark side

One
There has been too much indulgence of unsocial thoughts, too many dark encounters, to sit in tinseled rooms where everyone agrees on dualism and the right way.

The Other
"And to live there, among strangers,
Calls for teashop behaviours:
Setting down the cup,
Leaving the right tip...."
– Philip Larkin: *Strangers*

I
If you will not pretend, it may be better to avoid the bright rooms. But I must be watchful. To be wholly other-defined is to be sanitised; to be wholly self-defined is to be insane.

10. untold

One

One is the expectant face before the story begins. What story should be told, if any? Is not everything a kind of fiction? In here nothing is either true or false. The story will end in its beginning, because there is no plot and no inclination to fabricate a premise.

The Other

"One side says this, the other that. You work it out yourself
    and walk between the story lines.
What's true is what you do. Keep your head down. Know
    yourself. Ignore the starry skies."
– Ciaran Carson: *Two to Tango*

I

There's constant talk, and it only approximates meaning. Some say talking makes the mind. It's estimated that people talk to themselves ninety per cent of the time and to others the remaining ten. If this is so, it's probably what we tell ourselves that counts, and, plotted or not, becomes our story.

11. desert

One

A cold white desert permeates all things, becomes One, keeps One nameless. It is stuck to the cornea, piled in the ears, caravanned to the backbone.

The Other

"I speak of Desert without repose
Carved by relentless winds
Torn up from its bowels
Blinded by sands
Unsheltered solitary...."
– Andrée Chedid: *Landscapes*

I

We carry the world's phenomena as metaphors. They're part of us and we of them. Being thus of the mind, the white desert can't be escaped. But the mind's alchemy may transmute it. Sit. Let white be what white will. See if you die.

12. multifarious

One
All kinds of weather split One. Not to rainbow, but living slices in separate compartments. These are made of themselves and will not be adulterated, melded or alloyed.

The Other
"I disdain, I know, I do not know, I pursue, I laugh, I tyrannize, I protest.
I am philosopher, god, hero, demon and the whole universe."
– Heinrich Cornelius Agrippa von Nettesheim

I
The brain is a network of specialised loci that work separately but send signals everywhere—Daniel Dennett's 'pandemonium'. We feel that, don't we, you and I, as we stare at each other across this courtyard? But we're battling: against each, against all.

13. sotto voce

One
Speaking, it seems, though how to know? There is no echo, no discernible mode. One is the silent zone beneath the gunshot's report.

The Other
"And you O my soul where you stand,
Surrounded, detached, in measureless oceans of space,
Ceaselessly musing, venturing, throwing, seeking the
     spheres to connect them;
Till the bridge you will need be form'd, till the ductile
     anchor hold,
Till the gossamer thread you fling catch somewhere,
     O my soul."
– Walt Whitman: *A Noiseless Patient Spider*

I
What's heard depends on the hearer. The brain is like a hard drive and must be programmed. Without the appropriate 'software', one can't hear certain sounds, won't discern an audible language. Are you equipped to hear yourself? Are you speaking in the right place, with the right tone? How badly do you want to be heard? I hear you.

14. canvas

One
Receiving a puzzle of sense impressions. In a liminal state, still and somehow dispersed, One feels things come and go without name or definition. Like an interpretive instrument in no-body's hands.

The Other
"Now merely a lump of stone
smashed in the field of scythes,
a circle of calves around me
staring with silly eyes.
I lonesome like a haw tree
while lichen hones me down
and a lizard-brooch sleeps."
– Michael Hartnett: *The Naked Surgeon*

I
Walking into an art gallery, I'm ashamed to find myself thinking, *Who cares*? What are these creations but the ruts of a triumphalist species intent on perpetuating itself? Seeing through human culture to its animal core, I lose motivation. The sad island of scepticism gathers under my feet. This might be what's called depression. I call it insight and loneliness.

15. shapes

One
Each day is a visit to a theme park. Interact with the guides, learn a few attenuated facts, take part in didactic dramas, buy souvenirs. At closing time the coat is buttoned and polite goodbyes are exchanged. Once home, One does not know what has been experienced, if anything.

The Other
"The absurd is born of this confrontation between the human need and the unreasonable silence of the world. This must not be forgotten. This must be clung to because the whole consequence of a life can depend on it. The irrational, the human nostalgia, and the absurd that is born of their encounter—these are the three characters in the drama that must necessarily end with all the logic of which an existence is capable."
– Albert Camus: *The Myth of Sisyphus*

I
According to Friedrich Nietzsche, the ascetic is afraid of happiness and beauty, longs to get away from 'appearance, transience, growth, death'. Are you ascetic, or is it that, without an other to point out the meaning, your eyes glean nothing but shapes?

16. beast of burden

One
Tensions in the body, perennial anxieties, are One's lovers and friends. Every so often they depart, but One quickly calls them back for another round.

The Other
"What fear of revealing, of vulnerability, of being human, grips us so fiercely, and above all why? What unhealing wound, struck by what unimaginable betrayal, bleeds afresh when a hand of a loving friend is held out? What is it that, down there in the darkness of the psyche, cries its silent No to the longing for Yes?"
– Bernard Levin: *Enthusiasms*

I
You're perhaps burdened most by the feeling that you *must* be burdened, that comfort would be stealing what's not rightfully yours because it's not shared. But who'd know? Do I need to declare that you're sometimes untroubled, without stress or guilt, simply floating in a deep, undefining, nourishing pool of air?

17. am

One

Versions of self crowd in. Words lodge and will not unstick. *I am* is heard and there is turmoil, straining to equal the *I*, no matter its value.

The Other

"Humans routinely commit the logical fallacy of reification, turning an abstraction like 'democracy' into a hypostatized entity. That mental process has its uses, but it can also be misleading. We also routinely freeze dynamic events, like aspects of economics, biology, or physics, which might be dealt with more accurately with mathematical tools for dealing with fast-changing entities. Newtonian calculus was invented precisely to describe dynamic events that can be labelled by words in only a very impoverished fashion."

– Bernard J. Baars and Nicole M. Gage: *Cognition, Brain and Consciousness*

I

I create confusion, I know. I pick up epithets and place them in slots. They are most often derogatory and whip the self into better performance, or just whip the self. Unmediated, unargued by an other, they grow to concepts, then precepts, then barking gatekeepers.

18. twisted

One

Does One want to relinquish this intensity? Yes, it's pain to lie in bed twisted by shame at the harsh traits One has revealed, convinced that One is hated by workmates, terrified of the slightest creak in the dark. But each moment is full, the body reacts to every situation, the hairs on the arms are alert to each atmospheric shift. Reduce life to simple shared experience, or a joke, or manageable, and all sense of importance deflates.

The Other

"The experience of social isolation threatens our sense of purpose, which is one of the unifying factors in human development. It undermines the implicit bargain—self-regulation in exchange for social acceptance—on which personal identity is based, and which is one of the basic organizing principles of human society."

– John Cacioppo and William Patrick: *Loneliness*

I

Your aversion to the ordinary makes no sense. You're not so special. If anything, you're somewhat inept, shrinking from situations that might prove you so.

19. rampant

One
Emotion is unpredictable and fierce, a rampant elephant in a straw hut. Enemy and friend are equal targets. Unrestrained, One will smash the most precious exhibits of any museum.

The Other
"Our natural passions are few in number; they are the means to freedom, they tend to self-preservation. All those which enslave and destroy us have another source; nature does not bestow them on us; we seize on them in her despite."
– Jean-Jacques Rousseau: *Émile*

I
I can't see that I could seize on anything in 'despite' of nature. Nature is an inclusive continuum, not a discrete entity. I've evolved to what I am, so my passions can't be anything but natural, whatever their disguise. However, I must try to contain them if I'm to live in society. This is a battle I don't wish to fight.

20. puppet

One

There are chains of moments when One is captured from even deeper within, stolen by some non-event—the memory of a colour, an imagined drama. Hoisted by unseen, inexorable pulleys, One leaps in a random cause, speaks to no purpose.

The Other

"Let me give myself up entirely to the sweetness of conversing with my soul, since that is the only thing men cannot take away from me."

– Jean-Jacques Rousseau: *The Reveries of the Solitary Walker*

I

Rousseau's 'soul' is my body and the workings of my brain. How else could it be constituted? This conglomerate self is an industrious cellular community. Nothing that happens in here is a non-event.

21. witch

One
Witches were said to have red eyes and poor vision. One is a witch, unable to see through the head's inferno. In this age One will not be burned, but there are other, casual punishments.

The Other
"All solitude is selfish."
– Philip Larkin: *Vers de Société*

I
It could be argued that there's no reason to be alone in the twenty-first century, but that's to deny the stubborn nature of innate personality and the impact of trauma or broken relationships. Not to mention the element of chance. The chronically lone become more and more certain of their weirdness.

22. scroll

One

Days and nights gather like a curtain, opening and closing without reason. Ahead and behind are a series of stubborn puckers. One is the gap between them, the absence of a hand.

The Other

"Try as they may to savour the taste of eternity, their thoughts still twist and turn upon the ebb and flow of things in past and future time. But if only their minds could be fixed and steady, they would be still for a while and, for that short moment, they would glimpse the splendour of eternity, which is for ever still."

– Augustine of Hippo

I

The circle of light and dark is the binding on a formless text. Chapters, paragraphs, indents, colons, commas, exclamation marks, capital letters, full-stops: all these are alien to the scroll of the sun.

23. *tempus fugit*

One
How does One mark lone time? The rising and setting of celestial bodies are not enough when there is an inner orbit that wobbles, strays, slows and speeds, according to whim.

The Other
"... unlimited solitude that makes a lifetime of each day ... communion with the universe, in a word, space, the invisible space that man can live in nevertheless, and which surrounds him with countless presences."
– Rainer Maria Rilke: letter, quoted in Bachelard, *The Poetics of Space*

I
Solitary people often have rigid routines. They know where they'll be every day at three. This may sound unattractive, may fit all those negative reifications like 'compulsed', 'obsessive', 'dull', 'predictable', but it provides punctuation and structure. Unlike the socialite, the loner makes her own time.

24. mote

One
The week ahead is a blank, pallid sheet on some giant's bed. One is a microscopic mote among its fibres.

The Other
"At the moment we've got the habit of being unaware. We have to develop the habit of being present. Once we start to be present in the moment everything opens up. When we are mindful there is no commentary—it's a very naked experience, wakeful, vivid."
– Tenzin Palmo: *Cave in the Snow*

I
Will you now push me to make an arrangement, find a talk to attend, start a course, visit *Facebook*, do some housework, fill up my diary? Will that satisfy whatever question this condition is posing? Will we end up posed, masquerading as a human?

25. reflexive

One
Round and round, like a rolling hamster. No matter how One moves there is the circular bind—these arms, these knees, these hands, these toes, these arms, these knees, these hands, these toes, thesearmstheseknees thesehands....

The Other
"The communal ideal reckons without its host, overlooking the individual human being, who in the end will assert his claims."
– C. G. Jung: *The Undiscovered Self*

I
This chattering self-contemplation makes me both prisoner and jailor, the worst personal scenario. I wish I could vomit you—my self—as a snake does an eggshell. I can only try to assert, in time to our helpless roll, that I'll solve it or salve it, solve it or salve it....

26. stolen

One
When attention is invited to something outside, One is hampered by strident refrains, choked by associative memories, knocked out by the pitch and colours of a voice, a parcel of time stolen.

The Other
"I have a red light to keep me safe, like blood, when I go to the woods.... I go to the Blue Land, where the wind blows a lot, and bells make sounds, and people teach you things without saying a word."
– Diane Purkiss: *Troublesome Things*

I
Where is reality when dream is the norm? At least I'm aware of the difference between the inside and outside. Your 'red light' can be dimmed. I must not fear the stealing in of impressions, but add rather than subtract, find something tangible to capture me.

27. abdication

One
Usurp this voice. Let a coup take place in the small body politic, so that One might stop being conscious and astir.

The Other
"Thus let me live, unheard, unknown;
Thus unrepented let me die;
Steal from the world and not a stone
Tell where I lie."
– Alexander Pope: *Solitude: An Ode*

I
It seems a paradox to desire recognition and oblivion at the same time, but one often leads to the other. The self must be lost, not found. I can't be continually self-conscious and also content.

28. natural nothing

One
It is pathetic to have no companion but the beauty of nature;
to be reduced to remarking on the fineness of the day or the
phenomenon of a leaf; to have nothing livelier presenting to
Oneself than a walk in a park or wood. It is a life for the dying.

The Other
"I am monarch of all I survey,
My right there is none to dispute;
From the centre all round to the sea
I am Lord of the fowl and the brute.
O solitude! where are the charms
That sages have seen in thy face?
Better dwell in the midst of alarms,
Than reign in this horrible place."
– William Cowper: *The Solitude of Alexander Selkirk*

I
To see vegetation as personal company could be despair or
poetry, boredom or transportation. What prevents me from
achieving my notion of a full life? It seems I'm split between
desire and personality.

29. armoured

One
Although it causes pain, One resists groups. One will not speak their language, will walk One's own way. As though there were something valuable to lose, when there is so little in here that comforts or sustains.

The Other
"I will be myself alone.
Through the holes in the trellis
Falls thin rain. What drizzles
Slowly into my skull is this:

I will acclimatize.
My head will shrink in size."
– Ciaran Carson: *St Ciaran's Island*

I
The loner is as open as she is closed. The potential for invasion is so great that you must be armoured at all times. But the others have fears too, the greatest of which is the fear of being alone.

30. creature

One
Reach. Touch. Hold this shivering creature where it is crushed against the back wall of its cave. Stroke its head; say it is loved, free and unencumbered, can sleep in the open.

The Other
"The loner is like the branch cut from the tree that has to be grafted back on."
– Marcus Aurelius: *Meditations*

I
I shiver with you and can hardly speak. When you're like this, it's an effort to believe you're worthwhile, that the loner deserves to be comforted. I wonder if anything is deserved, and not simply snatched.

31. self-help

One
Crouched in the long grass, not waiting to pounce, but wondering when the world beyond the high green density will throw in a morsel.

The Other
"The revulsion from an unwanted self, and the impulse to forget it, mask it, slough it off and lose it, produce both a readiness to sacrifice the self and a willingness to dissolve it by losing one's individual distinctness in a compact collective whole."
– Eric Hoffer: *The True Believer*

I
Nobody will come. I have waited a long time and the meadow remains undisturbed by foot or hoof. I must make my own experience—hold myself like a beloved, groom myself like a prize horse, dress myself like a favourite child.

32. quiz

One

Each moment is a shower of poisoned questions. And still the others are dreaded, with whom One might shelter in answers.

The Other

"One cannot even begin to be conscious of oneself as a separate individual without another person with whom to compare oneself. A man in isolation is a collective man, a man without individuality."

– Anthony Storr: *The Integrity of the Personality*

I

If the real self could be gained through freedom from other people, then how is it that a 'self' in the human sense is not formed at all by isolated or wild children? The self is built by others and continues to evolve through interaction. Maybe your questions can be too easily answered, and what you fear is the loss of your special position in the sequestered domain.

jostled in a pixelated world

33. faithless

One
How to gain a companion? One can be kind and agreeable, but there is no combining. No other is suitable, because the internal universe demands perfection. When the ideal almost arises, One has no faith.

The Other
"Neither can I be angry with my brother or fall foul of him; for he and I were born to work together, like a man's two hands, feet, or eyelids, or like the upper and lower rows of his teeth. To obstruct each other is against Nature's law— and what is irritation or aversion but a form of obstruction?"
– Marcus Aurelius: *Meditations*

I
You build pictures without basis and demand the impossible. Rethink. Be positive about the other's existence as an equal. Accept your experience of yourself. Try to empathise. Don't underestimate. Be independent.

34. imagine

One
One smells flowers where there are none, sees faces in twilit houses, fancies voices in beckoning trees. One must not hallucinate. That would be total isolation, ignominy. At all costs, One must pretend to share the prevailing reality.

The Other
"[He] presently would note with despair that he had been unwary again and that a delicate move had just been made in his life, mercilessly continuing the fatal combination. Then he would decide to redouble his watchfulness and keep track of every second of his life, for traps could be everywhere. And he was oppressed most of all by the impossibility of inventing a rational defense, for his opponent's aim was still hidden."
– Vladimir Nabokov: *The Luzhin Defense*

I
The following experiences were recorded by Sara Maitland during her period of silence: intensification of physiological and psychological sensation; disinhibition; a sense of givenness or connection; auditory hallucinations; boundary confusions; exhilarating consciousness of being at risk; ineffability and bliss. Joe Simpson, alone and injured, high in the Peruvian Andes, heard voices, had mood swings, lost normal sense of time and fell into confused rituals of behaviour. Thomas Merton wrote of St. Francis seeing a seraph with fiery blood-red wings. Saints and the lone imagine.

35. centrifugally yours

One
One is not convinced by the seeming cohesion of groups. Beneath the posited unity there is a palpable straining of parts.

The Other
"... all peoples have a kind of centrifugal force that makes them continually act one against the other and tend to aggrandize themselves at their neighbour's expense, like the vortices of Descartes."
– Jean-Jacques Rousseau: *The Social Contract*

I
Social harmony is tenuous. Why else would all groups, from family to nation, be so manically focused on emblems of their unity? There are multitudinous versions of the flag: codes of dress; codes of speech; group-specific protocol. If they were natural friends, would they need such pummelling reassurance?

36. phantoms

One
Unable to rest in the absence, One invents a colourful coterie. Here's a lively conversant; here's a friend in need of advice; here's an attentive listener; here's a hand caressing, saying how gorgeous, patting One's hair like a mother-lover.

The Other
"To fight aloud is very brave —
But gallanter, I know
Who charge within the bosom
The cavalry of Woe — "
– Emily Dickinson: *126*

I
These imaginings thieve time and leave sadness in their wake. And still, without them would you forget what contact is? Remind yourself of the real phenomena, for fear of a dissociative state. Admit it's your own voice speaking, your own hand caressing, and not some phantom other.

37. callers

One
Always in some part preparing, organising, as though expecting an other to call. Who will not call. And then what are the preparations and arrangements but the vain shufflings of an eggless bird?

The Other
"I see life more as an affair of solitude diversified by company than an affair of company diversified by solitude."
– Philip Larkin: *New York Review of Books*

I
Many loners arrange their lives according to their solitude, making institutions of themselves. They grow rigid and dull-eyed, anxious, humourless. Nobody holds them. They don't make love.

38. one into many

One

How can One remain intact while with others? There is a tendency to be absorbed by the set of their mouths and the habits of their bodies. One turns away in desperation, fearing paralysis in the mobile face of time.

The Other

"The gradual inversion of meaning for the word 'individual', moving from the indivisible and collective to the divisible and distinctive, carries within itself the historical development of self-consciousness, testifies to that complex dynamic of change which separated the person from his world making him self-conscious and aware, that change in the structure of feeling which during the Renaissance shifted from a sense of unconscious fusion with the world towards a state of conscious individuation."

– Peter Abbs: *The Development of Autobiography in Western Culture*

I

People harangue each other into a definite stance and the expression of an 'individual self', but how individual is anybody? Psychologists can map developmental stages and even the most rebellious fit into them. The event of my birth and my particular genetic code are unique—I have no clone, am no clone—but my physical and psychological needs are fundamentally the same as those of others. It might be best to accept my humanity gracefully and then focus on my specific desires. Resistance might render me sliced, instead of indivisible.

39. sounding board

One

Tortured by chest aches and stomach churnings. The smallest of conflicts—the rasp of a voice, a passing cloud in the eye of an other—can cause sleepless weeks. One is a demented sounding board.

The Other

"People and animals that are sensorily deprived have an overly sensitized nervous system resulting in lowered thresholds to sensory stimuli."

– Temple Grandin: *Emergence: Labeled Autistic*

I

The human, like other animals, has a survival mechanism which needs to identify the location of an enemy or threat. A long period of isolation will strongly engage that mechanism. After all, you're your own protector, comprise the only home guard.

40. thought crime

One
One detests the hint of uniformity, argues with sentiment and group euphoria; homes in on the uglies of a face and the snags of a body. Unloves.

The Other
"At the crown-centre of oneself, [visualised] as Vajrasattva,
In the celestial palace of the blazing skulls, within one's brain,
Amidst an expanse of light composed of flaming seminal
     points of rainbow-light,
Is the assembly of blood-drinking deities, standing in clusters."
– *Tibetan Book of the Dead*

I
I've read enough books, watched enough movies, listened to enough conversations, to know that others have conflicting attitudes and malicious locations in their minds. Are your offences so huge?

41. selves

One

One sits listening when the sinews crave action; pays attention when thoughts reach elsewhere; helps when only disdain is felt; acts on advice though it is obviously flawed. The voice speaks of love without any understanding, chatters when the desire is for silence. Who is this? Where is the self?

The Other

"Insist on yourself; never imitate."
– Ralph Waldo Emerson: *Self-Reliance*

I

Without a solid sense of self, we fall prey to many pointless activities. Or so it seems. Scientists assert that the self is not locatable in any specific part of the brain, that it's not a monolithic entity. Could the tendency to frustrate our inclinations be an intrinsic part of our nature? If it weren't, would we do it? It may be truer to live contradiction than to attempt the construction of a monotone unit.

42. untouchable

One
Caution in the bodies of others. Is One's presence so forbidding? They never come close enough to look in. What would they find? A dugout, deep and silent, the floor flimsy as stretched muslin.

The Other
"Only a Bird will wonder —
Only a Breeze will sigh —
Ah little Rose — how easy
For such as thee to die!"
– Emily Dickinson: *35*

I
Your demeanour, developed in persistent solitude, might appear distant and forbidding; but even if this weren't so, your mind will accept no lodger. Neurological and genetic programming rule all; if your childhood and disposition had provided you with a sense of companionship, you'd hardly notice the lack.

43. preserve

One
How can others take their lives so lightly? Words are cast as though they were transiting dust, but One is speared and bleeds. After confrontation or close encounter, One remains in the spot, bound to the experience.

The Other
"As soon as something gets into the business of self-preservation, boundaries become important, for if you are setting out to preserve yourself, you don't want to squander effort trying to preserve the whole world: you draw the line. You become, in a word, selfish. This primordial form of selfishness (which, as a primordial form, lacks most of the flavors of our brand of selfishness) is one of the marks of life."
– Daniel Dennett: *Consciousness Explained*

I
Could I be like Camus' ideal man and elude nothing? This hypersensitivity crucifies, regardless. But if others don't feel it, is there need to feel it at all? I may be victim to some play of chemicals which has no purpose, a redundant programme. Let me try to contain your reactions as though they were pet tigers. Or transport them to where tigers can hunt.

44. equivocal

One
They demand enthusiasm. They are totally involved. They speak passion and immersion. They love—an other, a country, a subject, an activity. They plumb the eyes for something unequivocal. They will not find it. One pretends, or retreats into familiar solitude.

The Other
"I sit outside my own door
for four seasons.
I am tolerant of all weathers.
I see the leaf go back to the ground:
I am impartial to growth and death."
– Michael Hartnett: *Tao, 16*

I
Life is less a passion than a plod. I've attempted to immerse myself, but floundered in lack of faith and insufficient fact. From where I stand, the options are multifarious, each too valid for exclusion. Involvement makes one forget oneself. Excessive involvement makes one forget the world.

45. history

One
Their history is that of civilisation, how their ancestors won the ground, how they defended and expanded their territory, how they represented themselves in mirroring art. In here, history is of cellular origins, the power-play of elements, the enclosure of particles, how One functions according to One's own systematic rules.

The Other
"Light breaks where no sun shines;
Where no sea runs, the waters of the heart
Push in their tides...."
– Dylan Thomas: *Light Breaks Where No Sun Shines*

I
Are you so helpless in the face of your environment that you can't look to the wide world? Why not live both histories? Let's venture to claim our humanity before it's again dust in the microsphere.

46. extrovertible?

One

He's lovely. She's sweet. Look at him smile. Listen to her laugh. Cheer up! Be chatty! Be bubbly! Be down-to-earth. Ubiquitous banal exhortations to social cohesion. They are manic for assurance that One is safe and dirigible.

The Other

"Putting loners in busy workplaces all day is like making albinos pick cotton without sunscreen."
– Anneli Rufus: *Party of One*

I

It has been a source of surprise to me that many people who appear to be extrovert, who mingle a lot and smile incessantly at others, feel themselves to have very few friends and are burdened by many secrets.

47. company

One
Somebody is calling to the living place, but there will be no couple to greet them, no backdrop of friends to add validity. They will ask, *What do you do in your spare time? What music do you like? Do you enjoy living alone?* Answers must be prepared. All needs must be hidden for fear of driving them away.

The Other
"However mean your life is, meet it and live it; do not shun it and call it hard names."
– Henry David Thoreau: *Walden*

I
I'm spendthrift with my time, living events before and after they take place. To the observer I may appear unaccompanied, but I carry inside me all whom I contact and all my appointments. Not to mention you, Deep Chatterer, whom I must silence.

48. staying in

One
Home entertaining is a huge event. Everything else recedes in importance. The place must please them, One's dress must please them, One's demeanour must be acceptable. Sleep is lost. The visit is perfect. But it has all been adaptation and effort. Is this home?

The Other
"Only when compelled to act
am I entirely abandoned."
– Michael Hartnett: *Tao, 50*

I
I know a man who plans his solitary life so carefully that he'll refuse a social occasion to watch a football match. His life with himself is more important to him than a life which compromises for others. Another man who lives alone foregoes all engagements in order to get his apartment looking exactly the way he likes it. There must be a sense in them of the primary importance of their existence and individual will. Can we construct that, you and I—an internal partnership that, like a marriage, stands firm and self-satisfied in the social paradigm?

49. sartorial flunk

One
So often in ill-judged clothes. Not realising until afterwards, when an other remarks or there is a photograph, that they were garish or inappropriate.

The Other
"Einstein's dress and hair were typical of an adult with autistic tendencies, most of whom have little regard for social niceties and rank. When he worked at the Swiss patent office, he sometimes wore green slippers with flowers on them."
– Temple Grandin: *Thinking in Pictures*

I
Temple Grandin, an autistic scientist, had no idea how to dress for work until she was advised. That's not to say you're autistic. But perhaps lack of social definition means that you often choose what shines, in the moment, and not what will enhance you in a social setting.

50. zombie

One

Others speak of their lives. They say, *I am.... I can't bear.... I love....* These are statements One cannot complete. One is aware of no needs; and then of a huge, gaping wound. Self is as hidden as the dark heart of the other, the metal core of this unsettled earth.

The Other

"There was no one in him; behind his face (which even through the bad paintings of those times resembles no other) and his words, which were copious, fantastic and stormy, there was only a bit of coldness, a dream dreamt by no one."

– Jorge Luis Borges: *Everything and Nothing*

I

To be alone is to be without analogy. One is devoid of definitions, seeing the pixels and not the picture. Is this such a bad state? Beneath the talk, the drive to attain and acquire, there is always the precursor—consciousness without opinion. This could be the definition (the undefinition) of Nirvana.

51. unconventional

One

Why conform? In idiom, culture and social protocol, One is a maverick. Never engaged or comforted by these conventions, why should One feel it tragic when they are contravened?

The Other

"Divine am I inside and out, and I make holy whatever I
    touch or am touched from;
The scent of these arm-pits is aroma finer than prayer,
This head is more than churches or bibles or creeds."
– Walt Whitman: *Leaves of Grass*

I

Despite mass communication and common human nature, there are still a multitude of furrows. Dynamics vary greatly among groups, organisations and countries. A misplaced quotation mark is pain to the person for whom good grammar means personal achievement, but 'good grammar', 'good manners', are in themselves meaningless phrases. The wise person is the one who uses convention for its desirable ends, while remembering that it's practice-deep and culture-specific.

52. disinterest

One
In talk, One's own concerns are all that interest. Other topics are stillborn to the ears.

The Other
"Men descend to meet. In their habitual and mean service to the world, for which they forsake their native nobleness, they resemble those Arabian Sheiks who dwell in mean houses and effect an external poverty, to escape the rapacity of the Pacha, and reserve all their display of wealth for their interior and guarded retirements."
– Ralph Waldo Emerson: *The Over-soul*

I
Relationships are always tenuous, especially when there are strong needs and acute minds. I'm constantly divided between other people and my current obsession. They mutually diminish or exclude.

53. irrational

One
No words to frame a coherent philosophy, because this dark world has no clear view. Gagged by the alien logic of others, shocked into its fathomless maw.

The Other
"The reason nature is so great is that it has forgotten that it was chaos, but this thought can appear at any time."
– Søren Kierkegaard: *Either/Or, A Fragment of Life*

I
The true loner is embedded in nature. Unlike Beckett's dead voices in *Waiting for Godot*, to have lived is enough for him; he doesn't have to talk about it. Nature has its own voices beyond and beneath ears and tongues. But the uneasy loner squirms and deflates when he seeks validation and finds none. Or when she doesn't search at all, consumed by her body's bewildering events.

54. without end

One
Suggestions abound. *This is what you must.... You should....* But to what end? A happy humanhood, they say: a productive, constructive humanhood. One cannot fathom these terms.

The Other
"A meteor falls in the empty dark.
Someone is absent, the universe is bare —
listen, God. Are you there?"
– Michael Hartnett: *The Naked Surgeon*

I
Action might be an end in itself, though it's hard to find an activity that absorbs. What are the conditions for involvement? If I keep the eyes primed, maybe something will come within their sights to hold you.

55. assay

One
One is snagged on the spokes of their opinions, those minds sharpened on approval, gimlets of certainty. The woman is confident of her gifts, the man wins arguments.

The Other
"A man should learn to detect and watch that gleam of light which flashes from within, more than the lustre of the firmament of bards and sages. Yet he dismisses without notice his thought, because it is his."
– Ralph Waldo Emerson: *Self-reliance*

I
Ideas aren't safe houses; they're often forays into unknown territory. Come out of your frightened bind and try something untested. True certainty is a rare commodity, established, if ever, by experience. Action must precede it.

56. nowhere plans

One

Others say One is selfish, that if One is not socially involved, One is irrelevant, making 'nowhere plans for no-body'. The picture is true enough to mortify.

The Other

" 'Communication' (which always means talk) is the *sine qua non* of 'good relationships'. 'Alone' and 'lonely' have become almost synonymous; worse, perhaps, 'silent' and 'bored' seem to be moving closer together too."

– Sara Maitland: *A Book of Silence*

I

Who beyond one's self should one plan for? One's children, perhaps. Even these will very soon plan for themselves. On what basis can any sentient being be described as an absence?

57. unglossed

One
No native language. Suspended between the vernacular and the received, One speaks both and pretends to belong. Shocks the others by ending the sham with a snort, turns tail and disappears. Returns to a narrow trench in the head, gibbering and spent.

The Other
"With the moment of language the human gives itself up to the fabrication of its own world. For language brings the equivocal gift of self-consciousness."
– Michael Newton: *Savage Girls and Wild Boys*

I
There must be wisdom to be found in the spaces between words. Silence preceded me. Silence will take me back.

58. solecistic

One
One enters from the wings on the wrong side of the stage.
The mouth declaims unexpected lines. The cast is stumped.
The audience gasps and falls into a tense silence. What is
said cannot be unsaid. Retreat.

The Other
"A conversation begins
with a lie. And each

speaker of the so-called common language feels
the ice-floe split, the drift apart

as if powerless, as if up against
a force of nature...."
– Adrienne Rich: *Cartographies of Silence*

I
What happens spontaneously must have some rationale,
albeit one we don't understand. We can try to be noble, we
can try to speak the expected words, but Yeats was wrong in
his view that sufficient pretence amounted to reality. Your
nature remains, voiced or not.

59. prey

One
What is it that does the perceiving? Faces are easily forgotten, but One is profoundly aware of the quality of presence, the skin-altering tone of a voice, the signs in a body that speak stress or strength.

The Other
"So our ancestors have been equipped with a most valuable alarm system that would be triggered (mostly) whenever they were being *looked at* by another animal (Braitenberg, 1984). Identifying a predator at a (spatial) distance (instead of having to wait until you feel its teeth digging into you) is also a *temporally* more distal sort of anticipation: it gives you a head start at avoidance.

An important fact about such mechanisms is their discriminatory crudeness; they trade off what might be called *truth and accuracy* in reporting for speed and economy."
– Daniel Dennett: *Consciousness Explained*

I
I wonder if prolonged solitude in the early years leaves the brain more developed in the older regions that deal with fight or flight, the so called 'smell brain'. Temple Grandin points out that the amygdalae of autistic people are enlarged. Long lone periods at any stage in life can stimulate this brain area. It's more important to the amygdalae to assess a potential threat, therefore the feel of a presence, than to establish the proportions and aesthetic value of an other's appearance.

60. because you're mine

One

In intimacy, One claims ownership. Must be party to all decisions, the sole confidant, the anchor and oracle, *lares et penates*. The other must not have a stream of identity One cannot enter as a big fish.

The Other

"He was jealous of any male friends Linda had. He frequently accused her of cheating—once even taking her for a doctor's examination to confirm her virginity."

– Amy Turner: *Sunday Times* feature on Burt Pugach and Linda Riss

I

So the lover steps gingerly across your spun country, drugged by the power of your presence, always within sight, flightless. Is this a desirable state of affairs? Are you so compulsed that you can't behave otherwise, or can you choreograph your needs to a different set of movements? Because these will probably fail.

61. tragedy

One

One seeks out signs of unhappiness in the lives of others. They are almost always there. One's anxiety is somehow eased by the knowledge. Tragedy seems the truest of the genres.

The Other

"The act of self-denial seems to confer on us the right to be harsh and merciless towards others."
– Eric Hoffer: *The True Believer*

I

And still people laugh, declare love, say their lives are pleasurable. Do you dare examine these testimonies in your ferreting? Do you observe selectively in order to feed your taste for torture?

62. immiscible

One

A group of selves in a small space causes trembling. One retreats like a cornered animal. Will not change colour, even to camouflage. Not made to blend.

The Other

"I am my own only when I am alone. Apart from that I am the plaything of all those around me."

– Jean-Jacques Rousseau: *The Reveries of the Solitary Walker*

I

Why blend, if your inclination is otherwise? Why do you tremble? Look around, listen: there are echoes of your discomfort. Camouflage is a common social defence; retreat might be yours. Why not suit your purposes as others suit theirs?

63. or what?

One
One becomes chameleon, changes according to ambience and who is present. In a while becomes strained, empty again. Walks away struggling with ache, tears smarting behind the eyes.

The Other
"But nowhere have I found a home; I am unsettled in every city and I depart from every gate."
– Friedrich Nietzsche: *Thus Spake Zarathustra*

I
It could be illusion. You might belong as well as any other. Just that you keep saying no. Why? Because you're singing some wordless paean to an awkward gene? Because you're lost in fearful self-stroking? Or maybe you're right and you don't belong. Now what?

64. the worst

One
Hands itch to touch the breasts or genitals of an unwitting other. Dwelling on what is hidden and taboo. *The quiet ones are the worst*—a glib meme forever in the air. But true, because unexpectedly One turns perverse.

The Other
"Does an elementary life burn people down to elementary states, to pure anger, pure gluttony, pure sloth? Am I unfitted by my upbringing for a life of more complex feelings? Is that why I have never left the farm, foreign to townslife, preferring to immerse myself in a landscape of symbol where simple passions can spin and fume around their own centres, in limitless space, in endless time, working out their own forms of damnation?"
– J. M. Coetzee: *In the Heart of the Country*

I
Taboo impulses are recurrent subjects for comedy, so they must be commonly felt. The human mind is far from pure. Your guilt is as much a problem as your lewd imagining.

65. avaricious

One
Ambition is a hurricane that devours the needs of others. It seems there is always somebody who will be displaced. To avoid resentment or revenge, One chokes the stronger impulses as they rise. They do not die. They remain gasping and savage, shackled in a subterranean cave.

The Other
"The aim of life is self-development. To realize one's nature perfectly—that is what each of us is here for. People are afraid of themselves, nowadays. They have forgotten the highest of all duties, the duty that one owes to one's self."
– Oscar Wilde: *The Picture of Dorian Gray*

I
In contemporary western society, the emphasis is on satisfying desires and expressing one's self. In such a culture, the common interest is served by individual ambition. Trapped inside, it might seem you have the power of extreme weather and are unbearably arrogant, but there are many who are more powerful and will serve their own goals without hesitation.

66. no midas

One
The leaden touch. Everything tarnishes. Lovers are hurt, children set adrift. Abandoned friends are shocked and disillusioned. Casual encounters turn deathly serious. One is the bringer of conflict.

The Other
"I am crude, sullen, impolite on principle, and I want no one to fawn on me; so I will speak the truth quite unhampered."
– Jean-Jacques Rousseau: *Last Reply*

I
The chief sin of Camus' outsider is that he refuses to lie. Deception and diplomacy are essential to social harmony; venting unmediated impulses can lead to fractures. If I live my nature, I'll be a cauldron brimming with poisons and cures. Curb it, and I'll be a weak, unremarkable cup of tea.

67. manoeuvres

One
Unallied. The other's mind is enemy territory. No matter how much they reassure of their allegiance, the smallest sign of disloyalty and One's battle-lines are re-drawn.

The Other
"The psycho-analyst Erik Erikson has postulated basic trust versus basic mistrust as the earliest nuclear conflict which the developing human being encounters."
– Anthony Storr: *Solitude*

I
Consider the possibility that practice and programming overrides facts. Your distrust might be a non-appropriate, programmed fear response. Assess the threat. What exactly can the other take from you?

68. imperfect

One
Close-up, faces are rough and unhoned territory. Speech and composure are rarely perfect. Even when there is beauty and clever phrasing, there are unsatisfying ideas, notions that are not thought through, knowledge half-learned. Nothing completes.

The Other
"Excellence, here [in the Cistercian Monastery], was in proportion to obscurity: the one who was best was the one who was least observed, least distinguished. Only faults and mistakes drew attention to the individual."
– Thomas Merton: *Seven Storey Mountain*

I
Like any prisoner, your life is made more bearable by enumerating the flaws in the world outside. Your own imperfections complete the picture.

69. those pernicious others

One
They are engrained in the harsh tongue of the mirror. They watch One's movements with particulate eyes. Every nerve of the others is connected to a mind that knows the littlest of these thoughts. Little One.

The Other
"I have become solitary, or, as they say, unsociable and misanthropic, because to me the most desolate solitude seems preferable to the society of wicked men which is nourished only by betrayals and hatred."
– Jean-Jacques Rousseau: *The Reveries of the Solitary Walker*

I
Loneliness is associated with a threat or adrenaline-like pattern of activation of the stress response, coupled with high blood pressure. Flooded by such stimuli, we scramble for verbal correlatives and frequently find the wrong ones. Others don't know our thoughts. How could they? No floodlight sweeps the brain for signs of mutiny.

70. green-eyed

One

The success of others curries desire for sabotage. Cannot understand the sharing of joys. Malice rises like a starved tongue and can only be restrained by will-force.

The Other

"All health and success does me good, however far off and withdrawn it may appear; all disease and failure helps make me sad and does me evil, however much sympathy it may have with me or I with it. If, then, we would indeed restore mankind by truly Indian, botanic, magnetic or natural means, let us first be as simple and well as Nature ourselves, dispel the clouds which hang over our own brows, and take up a little life into our pores."

– Henry David Thoreau: *Walden*

I

Are you not also successful in some way? Can you set your own standards and make satisfaction your saviour? But you have the nature of a tyrant, who rules by diminishment.

71. *a priori*

One

Earliest memory: lying prone in a cot. There is the broad face and wild hair of a woman above. She is smiling eagerly and making strange sounds she presumes the baby will like. One judges her silly and intrusive. Starts to bawl.

The Other

"What sort of space is that which separates a man from his fellows and makes him solitary? I have found that no exertion of the legs can bring two minds much nearer to one another."

– Henry David Thoreau: *Walden*

I

And so it began, this perennial disaffection. Even as a baby you were exacting tribute from your environment, demanding that others live up to some impossible standard. If the trait is ingrained, then I suppose I must behave as I might with any other handicap—manage it with mindfulness, responsibility or drugs. Get a personality prosthesis.

72. shadow-boxing

One

Liar, deceiver. Your intent is clear. Come on. Just try it. There is strength in here you cannot imagine. One will survive your worst, hauling the wounded parts, broken but doing.

The Other

"Shall I unbolt or stay
Alone till the day I die
Unseen by stranger-eyes
In this white house?
Hands, hold you poison or grapes?"
– Dylan Thomas: *Ears in the Turrets Hear*

I

The word 'paranoia' is derived from the Greek *para*, meaning 'beside', and *noos* meaning 'mind'. If I'm not quite out of my mind, the mind I'm in is distorting. The others might have no problem with the fact of your existence. They may well be indifferent to you.

73. beyond compare

One

Cruelly comparing Oneself. Who is the most clever, attractive, good? Try to diminish the impact of others by avoiding those who are patently superior. One will die this way, worthless.

The Other

"Public opinion is a weak tyrant compared with our own private opinion."

– Henry David Thoreau: *Walden and Civil Disobedience*

I

Modern man, said Jung, is a fictive personality with a shadow instinctual side. I see this conflict in the dynamics of every group. Try to be generous, and if that's not possible, be diplomatic. Smile. Leave early.

74. cowed

One
Terrified that honesty will reveal One to the others as deficient. One is cowed by the prospect of ridicule, a disgusted turning away, their possession of something One's nature cannot grasp.

The Other
"It is easy in the world to live after the world's opinion; it is easy in solitude to live after one's own; but the great man is he who in the midst of the crowd keeps with perfect sweetness the independence of solitude."
– Ralph Waldo Emerson: *Self-reliance*

I
Others can neither understand nor live my life. Why then do I give them so much power? In my lone times, can I fill my ambience with my own choices, build a structure? It seems that friends come when they're least craved.

75. unlook

One
One avoids the meeting of other eyes; cannot conceal the deep dissent, resistance to assimilation, the strength of these uncivilised passions.

The Other
"It has been said that the great events of the world take place in the brain. It is in the brain, and the brain only, that the great sins of the world take place also."
– Oscar Wilde: *The Picture of Dorian Gray*

I
Damn you. You keep me from the joy of company with your constant self-obsessed whisperings. Like the spider who eats the light, you devour the vistas I could savour.

76. placing

One
One analyses without pause, labours to reduce the others to principles. They are unreadable, infuriating. Only in family is there inalienable belonging, each person placed, like members of a phalanx.

The Other
"Why not admit that other people are always
  Organic to the self, that a monologue
Is the death of language and that a single lion
  Is less himself, or alive, than a dog and another dog?"
– Louis MacNeice: *Autumn Journal*

I
Complete control might be attainable by the unscrupulous, but do you want such a weighty characteristic? You must allow others their place beyond your ken, as their lives are beyond your experience. Family will not always suffice.

77. untested

One
Why don't they batter the walls, break through One's defences? In battle One could test mass, volume and level of strength, but in this impassive space One is the only number, therefore no number, powerless.

The Other
"Her wits were turned with solitude and freedom. No one checked her. No one taught her."
– Virginia Woolf: *A Room of One's Own*

I
The mind needs shocks to assist it in breaking through to reality, the Zen master, D. T. Suzuki, once said. These shocks may get their power from intense emotional excitement. But what if the shocks never come; if the prevailing condition in one's life is absence? Then, I suppose, one must create one's own obstacles and challenges. Or, by accepting an untested state, learn if it's freedom or apathy.

78. balance

One

Everything learned alters One, like a tablet dropped into water. The colour changes, the chemical constitution is affected. But others learn and still maintain the established track. What they know changes nothing, upsets nothing. They are balanced apple carts, gliding on an even road.

The Other

"Let us thank God for valour in abstraction
For those who go their own way, will not kiss
The arse of law and order nor compound
For physical comfort at the price of pride."
– Louis MacNeice: *Eclogue from Iceland*

I

There are others like you, but in the manner of a cat, you don't associate. Change has been effected by alterable people. I don't want to be impervious or set. I want to wobble with you on the cobblestones, even overturn.

sent from the throat of a wind

79. portable community

One
This is community enough, this tidal place, wave drawing wave, drops jostling each other. Eddies and currents have their own will, thinking themselves oceans or even whole worlds.

The Other
[The inert gases are] "so inert, so satisfied with their condition, that they do not interfere in any chemical reaction, do not combine with any other element, and for precisely this reason have gone undetected for centuries."
– Primo Levi: *The Periodic Table*

I
A person is a walking co-operative, a multitude of inner congregations labouring at their separate tasks. Is this the reality you touch when you're absorbed in your storms? Or is it that chronic anxiety has made a virtue of turbulence?

80. aimless

One

No deadlines or appointments. Nothing that must be done. Fainting inside. As aimless and unshaped as the constituents of air.

The Other

"What are we when we are alone? Some, when they are alone, cease to exist."
– Eric Hoffer: *Reflections on the Human Condition*

I

Beyond my constructed activities and goals, there's an immense world in which there are no aims or plans, only mindless compulsions. That world is death to my consciousness, but its components are my components, its sustenance my sustenance. When I'm less 'human' I'm more 'world'.

81. *ab origine*

One

Nothing is true in itself. All theories are flawed, all disciplines limited. For a time One is captivated; then the rationale and structuring become obvious and the thoughts are not so fine, not a conduit for the pure. The essence is always elsewhere.

The Other

"It was not the absence of everything that I felt, but the presence of Nothing."
– George MacDonald: *Lilith*

I

The only truism is that there's no truth, because the essence of things is beyond human grasp. How can this body comprehend what is not native to senses and is of a grandly multifarious source? Your yearning is both a boon and a curse—you're not fixed, but you're never at home.

82. unmade

One
One hears talk of identity, demands for coherence. Viewed from here, there are only segments of experience, functions, moments of awareness. No monadic entity. One is a piece of clay forever slopping on the wheel.

The Other
"But this ambiguity of our being does not rest upon a self-existing unity, otherwise we could be conscious of ourselves in ourselves, and independent of the objects of knowledge and will. Now this is simply impossible, for as soon as we turn into ourselves to make the attempt, and seek for once to know ourselves fully by means of introspective reflection, we are lost in a bottomless void; we find ourselves to be the crystal ball out of which a voice speaks whose cause is not to be found in it, and wanting to understand ourselves, we grasp, with a shudder, only an insubstantial spectre...."
– Arthur Schopenhauer: *The World as Will and Idea*

I
There is no unchangeable core. If my mental faculties were taken away, one by one, each subtraction would alter my personality. My body, which is my primary definition, will finally transform into derivative substances and entities. However I try to shape myself, I can never be complete, nor should I.

83. the orienting stone

One

They wonder why One has no strong desire to travel widely or frequent popular social venues. They say One is not living. But One feels at the core a still, meditating stone that orients. Too often shifted, it might erode to a pebble; then nothing at all.

The Other

"If I were confined to a corner of a garret all my days, like a spider, the world would be just as large to me while I had my thoughts about me."

– Henry David Thoreau: *Walden*

I

How desirable is normal behaviour? We have a large interior life. It might survive amid noise, speed and the demand for explanations, but it will certainly be compromised. What happens when you open your inners might ease psychological strain, but is it the world?

84. bad

One

One is bad. Not working as many others do, who sacrifice their health and appearance in the interest of the common good. They pursue the best in morality and performance, adapt themselves. One lives carefully but without ideology, strives for excellence, not for the race, but for its own sake.

The Other

"Let him (the youth) know that man is by nature good, let him feel it, let him judge his neighbour by himself; but let him see how men are depraved and perverted by society; let him find the source of all their vices in their preconceived opinions; let him be disposed to respect the individual, but to despise the multitude; let him see that all men wear almost the same mask, but let him also know that some faces are fairer than the mask that conceals them."

– Jean-Jacques Rousseau: *Émile*

I

Regardless of your intention, the notion of excellence serves the race well in evolutionary terms. Comparing our performance with that of others, setting standards to be reached, keeps us striving, developing new skills, reinforcing old ones. The word 'bad' may have derived from the Middle English derogatory term *bæddel* meaning 'effeminate man', 'hermaphrodite', 'pederast'. That the reproduction imperative might be the source of this word makes it an appropriate epithet for you, not sure if you care whether the race is perpetuated or not.

85. in spirit

One
It happens without plan. A scenario, a whole event, plays itself out in the head. It causes excitement, joy, tears—all those emotions that are gained from intimacy and community. This is experience too.

The Other
"An absolute silence leads to sadness. It offers an image of death. Then the assistance of a cheerful imagination is necessary and comes naturally enough to those whom Heaven has favoured. Movement which does not occur from outside then occurs inside us."
– Jean-Jacques Rousseau: *The Reveries of the Solitary Walker*

I
Daydreaming is a port where we can shelter from trying time and repetitive tide, but we can't stay there or we might be outcasts forever. I'm trying with all my might to resist inventing a god.

86. mosaic

One
To socialise is to be cut into small shapes and set in mortar.
With such a scatter One cannot feel One's own colours.

The Other
"Just think of all the spare time that has flown

Straight into nothingness by being filled
With forks and faces, rather than repaid
Under a lamp, hearing the noise of wind,
And looking out to see the moon thinned
To an air-sharpened blade."
– Philip Larkin: *Vers de Société*

I
People relish social buzz. It's an achievement to have
multiple contacts, be part of some cultural set. I find myself
standing apart, preserving your unplaceable accent in the
pattern of voices.

87. still

One
Some mornings One is a calm channel for all sentient streams and contains, even transforms, conflict.

The Other
"All compounded beings lack permanence. Their essence is empty and selfless."
– *Tibetan Book of the Dead*

I
Weather pours into the sensitised, changes the attitude. It's a surprise to find you devoid of storms, still as a cave-lake, when yesterday you were spinning with a wild wind.

88. safe and sorry

One
The day will bring no surprises from the plastic and eventing mind of an other. Such order. Such iron security.

The Other
"I find it wholesome to be alone the greater part of the time. To be in company, even with the best, is soon wearisome and dissipating. I love to be alone. I never found the companion that was so companionable as solitude."
– Henry David Thoreau: *Walden*

I
It's hard to begin when the starting point is small and unsupported. Thoughts are unchallenged and unadmired, decisions have no dialogue to make them sound. But if I acquire a pet, talk to the television, perform work that would please an absent parent, build a routine, am I making my solitude even less pregnable?

89. criminal

One
Perfectly free. What action is not possible? Illicit love affairs, embezzlement, even murder. Crime is simple when there are no unshiftable loyalties and nobody to hamper or distract.

The Other
"Retreat into yourself, but first prepare to receive yourself; it would be madness to trust oneself to one's own rule, if one knew not how to govern. It is just as possible to err alone as it is in company."
– Michel de Montaigne: *Of Solitude*

I
There may be no universal morality, but there are contexts and consequences. Usually the consequences of erring are too great, even for those without close relationships. Do you want the world to view you as pernicious? Without a bolstering army, you are hardly big or strong enough to stand alone and despised.

90. bored

One

Bored by the plod, this halting mode of existence, the lack of ambient story. Others have urgent engagements, relevant witticisms, the inclination to stay late at parties, keep dancing.

The Other

"... the pain resulting from boredom is compounded by the physical effects of crowding. When an electron is confined in too small a space, it goes 'berserk'. Its position becomes too fixed, and thus the Uncertainty Principle (we can't know both a particle's position and its momentum) requires that its momentum become too great. Being quantum systems, conscious systems suffer similarly from too much crowding."
– Danah Zohar: *The Quantum Self*

I

Boredom has two components: disinterest and containment. The one is spontaneous, the other imposed. Is it that you've little interest in the life presented to you? Habitual solitude has reduced your ability to find entertainments, but your environment is replete with them, and your streets are not patrolled. I must conclude that you lack the resource of curiosity and the confidence to veer from beaten tracks.

91. redundant hero

One
Is there any use for anger in a time of peace? One disrupts for no reason. If there were war, One could easily take the shape of a hero and pit everything against the odds. But it would not be heroic, because One has nothing so precious that it cannot be sacrificed.

The Other
"The self thrown back on itself, with nothing but itself as a source of meaning, truth and value, has no nourishment on which to draw. It is like a plant that has been potted in a box in the garden shed rather than outside in the soil and sunlight. Very soon its roots dry up and its leaves wither. There must be something beyond ourselves to give those selves a sense of what we are about."
– Danah Zohar: *The Quantum Self*

I
There is scope for heroism in peace-time. I could join a humanitarian organisation, climb a mountain, play a sport. At least exercise. Strenuous activity induces a 'challenge' pattern of high blood flow and cardiac output, focusing the energy and drive. I know the theory, I seek the motivation.

92. behave

One

Can One eat olives for breakfast, soak in films all day, paint the walls red and the ceilings blue, bury Oneself in repetitive acts? Whose standards are correct? It is paralysing, not knowing how to behave.

The Other

"The logic of worldly success rests on a fallacy: the strange error that our perfection depends on the thoughts and opinions and applause of other men! A weird life it is, indeed, to be living always in somebody else's imagination, as if that were the only place in which one could at last become real!"

– Thomas Merton: *The Seven Storey Mountain*

I

Are you so fragile and unsure that you can fix on nothing unless an other approves? Why invite a tyrant to your table, when of all people you could be a free agent?

93. triggers

One

This: the cryptic puzzle on a day's front page and the dog pawing to distraction. This: the repair man arriving, to spoil the prospect of a slow breakfast. This: a milk carton toppling, while the limbs still hanker for the sheath of oblivion. A glass shatters on the tiles. One kicks the bin. One wants to kick: dog; repair man; glass; every eager face that asks the predictable questions.

The Other

"Some research has been done on the premise that violence may be related to inadequate somatosensory stimulation."
– Temple Grandin: *Emergence: Labeled Autistic*

I

There's something very wrong with my life when I can't address simple issues without an element of panic. Time closes in like a tunnel. People close in like hostile soldiers.

94. futile

One

One works hard, attends to detail, holds to routine. It is futile. There is no arbiter, no approver, no dependant on this presence. The work could be done by an other just as well. One grows careless and sullen, makes deliberate mistakes, drugs Oneself oblivious.

The Other

"Always be mindful that your pursuits will maintain their integrity as long as they are of worth to you. Remember he who, when asked why he toiled so hard on a task that only had significance for a scant amount of people, replied: 'A few, or one, or even none is plenty'. He speaks the truth; you and one companion are sufficient company, each for the other, as indeed you are for yourself. Let a crowd consist of one, and one be a crowd."

– Michel de Montaigne: *Of Solitude*

I

If we obtain the approval of others, it's usually because our actions are beneficial to them or the race. We're programmed to keep moving and to produce. All activity is survival or its metaphors. I might accept what my nature proclaims as its needs, decide on priorities and *modus operandi*, seek no affirming seal.

95. self-ish

One

Is there merit or sense in living just for Oneself? A good meal is prepared, the living space is decorated, the skin is bathed and oiled. Without an other to appreciate, these seem like pathetic, empty acts.

The Other

"What is the point of maintaining a body that no one touches? And why would you choose a nice hotel bedroom if you have to sleep there alone? I could only, like so many who had finally been defeated despite their sniggers and their grimaces, bow down: immense and admirable, undoubtedly, was the power of love."

– Michel Houellebecq: *The Possibility of an Island*

I

What's done alone seems halved in value and gives rise to ache. But the parameters of value are ill-defined. Could I adopt the Buddhist or absurdist approach, allowing all phenomena an underlying emptiness? Then my actions would be worthwhile and worthless, performed with equanimity. I might even be happy. Feeling into each moment like an exploring child.

96. in-ventures

One

Bears are concepts; tigers documentaries; mountains Michael Palin and Joe Simpson. Little is touched that is physically dangerous. Instead, One delves and scrapes the bottom of this well, finding within its seamless wall quakes, marshes, a terrifying wormhole.

The Other

"I complain that in life it is not as in the novel, where one has hardhearted fathers and nisses and trolls to battle, and enchanted princesses to free. What are all such adversaries together compared with the pale, bloodless, tenacious-of-life nocturnal forms with which I battle and to which I myself give life and existence."

– Søren Kierkegaard: *Either/Or, A Fragment of Life*

I

Kierkegaard was writing in the 1840s, when, in other streams of experience, people were battling against hardhearted landlords and the nisses and trolls of starvation. Liberty was often the enchanted princess. Can one complain of 'nocturnal forms' when so many others are neither fed nor physically safe? Can one rummage in the internal when others can only think of their next meal? If I believed in a destined purpose, I might say that we do what we must.

97. stalked

One

There is a sense of being followed. A figure watches the house from across the road. There is no outline, but the presence embosses the air like a dark, indelible burn.

The Other

" *'Mein Sohn, was birgst du so bang dein Gesicht?'* —
'Siehst, Vater, du den Erlkönig nicht?
Den Erlenkönig mit Kron und Schweif?' —
'Mein Sohn, es ist ein Nebelstreif.' "

" 'My son, why is your face so appalled?' —
'The Erlking, Father, don't you see him at all?
The Erlking with crown and cloak?' —
'My son, it's a strip of fog.' "
– Johann Wolfgang von Goethe: *Erlkönig / Erlking*

I

Isolation can lead to distortion of images and impairment of colour perception. It may also induce results usually attributed to drugs such as mescaline and lysergic acid. The ability to concentrate deteriorates, the mind becomes lethargic. In this state, false perceptions are hard to shake. I must keep saying, as in a movie, *He's not there, he's not there.* It's only my malfunctioning parietal lobe.

98. threshold

One

Comes in, locks the door and sits. One sometimes calls this place home, but it is a dull dwelling—small, unadorned. Like an animal's lair, perhaps? No, because One is less safe here than in the open. The eye of a reptile dawns before the face, not in pursuit but in possession.

The Other

"Felice, beware of thinking of life as commonplace, if by commonplace, you mean monotonous, simple, petty. Life is merely terrible; I feel it as few others do. Often—and in my inmost self perhaps all the time—I doubt whether I am a human being."

– Franz Kafka: *Franz Kafka: Letters to Felice*

I

For as long as I'm solitary, how can I see my habitat as anything other than a way station? The finer points of living are social. It appears I'm still on the threshold of my own species.

99. the fearsome dark

One

The dark is voracious as the Atlantic Ocean. Cannot climb the stairs without a light behind and before. Thank the benevolent god, Electricity, for birthing One in his time. Needling through night up the spiralled steps of castles, it would have taken many meetings with sweethearts and stolen kisses to steady the feet.

The Other

"Cold and darkness deplete a body gradually; the mind turns sluggish; the nervous system slows up.... Try as I may I cannot take my loneliness casually. It is too big. But I must not dwell on it. Otherwise I am undone."

– William Byrd: *Alone*

I

Even on warm nights, your fraught relationship with the dark makes me shiver. I face its unknown without companion or sword, and may never return.

100. rack

One

Will the torture never cease? Prostrate on the floor, pinned by the ocean-weight of silence. How can One be so burdened by absence? How can it have mass, move quick or sluggish as it likes, lay snares, tripwires, spancel the feet, pull down on the coat-tails, deafen with its raking, toneless voice?

The Other

"keep me from the vast returnings ...
returning of flesh into weals
returning of salt to my scars
returning of fears of the night
returning of pain of the gorse-gash ...
I can be broken no more."
– Michael Hartnett: *Short Mass*

I

No prospect. Nothing to be done. The world has shrunken to the size of the body. I'm clasped tight to you, but you're comfortless. Whether I survive or not is of no matter. All I know is the hard floor and a fathomless hunger of which I am the dry, toothless mouth.

101. prospect

One
To have been a phenomenon; to have risen to the brim with emotion and the poisoned blood of unstanched thought; to have worked well and badly; to have melted in sadness and moltened in rage; to have been stupid and wise; to have agonised in the cause of truth; to have discarded truth; to have punished the body and tortured the consciousness in pursuit of an unadulterated act; and to die irrelevant, no other having come within sight of the depth. The prospect brings tears upon tears.

The Other
"I do not know what is untried and afterward,
But I know it is sure and alive and sufficient.

Each who passes is considered, and each who stops is considered, and not a single one can it fail."
– Walt Whitman: *Leaves of Grass*

I
I have been a phenomenon. Somebody has seen me, dim or distinct. The chemicals of the air are close to me; I affect them. My form has made an impact on the surface of the earth, my thoughts have sent signals. Relationship is not always body to body, lip to lip, grammar to grammar. I know this, but I don't believe, because I'm a reluctant wanderer, wishing for lights from the dwellings of my own kind.

PART 2: THE DANGEROUS WORLD

The Other

Bridgie doesn't know that she's alive.
She carries her flesh like the dark load
heaped in baskets on a donkey's back.

She sees her likeness nowhere, nor her opposite.
When at times a mirror begins, she buckles with fear
and smashes it before it becomes form.

Goes back then to where she has no name,
a place that when oblivious was bed,
but self-conscious is a spiked and contracting cell.

Evicted, she walks the narrow corridor
between name and its absence, not seeing the others,
believing herself the only one without grasp

of this inaccurate map that is the body,
hiding from eyes that think they can define
her source, her measure and her meaning.

the dark load

102. instress

The Other
"My mother groaned, my father wept,
Into the dangerous world I leapt;
Helpless, naked, piping loud,
Like a fiend hid in a cloud."
– William Blake: *Infant Sorrow*

One
The first birth-light burning still stresses the eyes. May they never become accustomed to the light, so that it is always a shock, reminder of borders and what is wild.

I
Conflict is a creative force. Birth in itself is conflict, one organism expelling another. Our light is stolen from the darkness. Live the contradiction.

103. shaping forces

The Other
"There is in us a tendency to locate the shaping forces of our existence outside ourselves."
– Eric Hoffer: *The True Believer*

One
This eremitic life is not a choice. One longs to be an object of attention, to belong to some group, to be needed in dialogue. But attention cannot be held to this, and friends depart to their fuller lives. The lone state comes round and round like the relentless dawn.

I
We're not of our own making. Scientists are discovering more and more ways in which genes rule the roost. Let's say we're involved with the shaping forces, because they must express themselves through us, but the architectural decisions are not ours.

108. leper

The Other
"... when men reduced me to living alone, I found that by sequestering me to make me more miserable, they had done more for my happiness than I had ever been able to do."
– Jean-Jacques Rousseau: *The Reveries of the Solitary Walker*

One
The world draws back as though One were a cosmic leper, stunted and abandoned in a shadowless field, seared by the indifferent sun.

I
When all the connections are broken and sound is honed to a hum, there's a voiceless, pulsing insistence claiming life as its own self. You may ride with it or not. Exclusion is its own brand of freedom.

109. speak

The Other

"An der bildung ist mir nichts gelegen
denn ich bin der Feuerregen
und mein Blick ist, wie der Blitz gezackt."

"I am careless with the forms of creation
because I am the fire-filled rain
and my glance is pronged, like lightning."
– Rainer Maria Rilke: *The Words of the Lord to John on Patmos*

One

What is there to be or achieve? One is exhorted to have goals, work hard, take pride in a task well done. But neither personal attainment nor altruistic projects are enough to absorb this slow, barbed eye that sees only a language telling itself it is the truth.

I

Deconstruction is the way of the melancholy and the lone. Sometimes it's a product of the state of mind, sometimes it's the cause. Being your way, it's also what you are. What can a language do but speak?

110. horror

The Other
"The Horror not to be surveyed —
But skirted in the dark —"
– Emily Dickinson: *777*

One
One has known darkness in the extreme, has felt the self as
non-human, an entity as perfidious as a virus. This demands
to be remembered, howls at any attempt to bury it.

I
I carry my yesterdays on my back like a beaten animal. No,
I'm not nice. Who is? The teeming conglomeration that con-
stitutes a body is as nice and as un-nice as any ecosystem.
But I'm sorry. I'm so sorry that I wake in the middle of the
night with my heart pounding, hating its relentless tenacity.
I want to hurt myself but don't have the guts. The nearest I
go is to cut my hair. I snip it every which way. I look a fright.
Now will they see?

111. thin air

The Other
"[the] ideal potential convert [to a mass movement is] the individual who stands alone, who has no collective body he can blend with and lose himself in and so mask the pettiness, meaninglessness and shabbiness of his individual existence."
– Eric Hoffer: *The True Believer*

One
Every so often One becomes painfully aware of the multitude of others and One's own irrelevance. The mind is a small unit. The wide world will dispose of what happens in here.

I
So, will you cushion yourself with belief and social involvement? It would be a kind of resolution. Or you could burn the cushions, sit on the hard floor, embrace the thin air.

116. the source

The Other
"I was so distinctly made aware of the presence of something kindred to me, even in scenes which we are accustomed to call wild and dreary, and also that the nearest of blood to me and humanest was not a person nor a villager, that I thought no place could ever be strange to me again."
– Henry David Thoreau: *Walden*

One
Hankering after the first thing, the source, not its proliferating definitions. The search is physical. One wants to know the principles in the body, dance-feel-sound them.

I
If the source is to be understood, it must be by the un-speaking parts of the physical experience. The mind seeks to reduce this pre-linguistic knowing to concepts. When you decompose into elements, you'll know without thought. Meanwhile you can dance close and let the fingers of infinity play in your hair.

117. infused

The Other

"There is one mind common to all individual men. Every man is an inlet to the same and to all of the same. He that is once admitted to the right of reason is made a freeman of the whole estate. What Plato has thought, he may think; what a saint has felt, he may feel; what at any time has befallen any man, he can understand. Who hath access to this universal mind is a party to all that is or can be done, for this is the only and sovereign agent."
– Ralph Waldo Emerson: *History*

One

Role and relation are never fixed. One settles where dropped, fizzes in the alembic of a sad story, believes Oneself culprit and hero. Surprisingly particulate in group euphoria, panic, a deeply sung song.

I

The Buddhists aspire to formlessness, but all form will ultimately be lost. True, the consciousness is happier when it's capable of rising above the chaos and pain of emotion, but why should we reject any experience, when everything has its end? Can we not say yes to the wave and yes to the sea and yes to being here, now, imprisoned and liberated by form? Would you feel the unity if you weren't separate?

118. soluble

The Other
"… not a valve, not a wall, not an intersection is there anywhere in nature, but one blood rolls uninterruptedly an endless circulation through all men, as the water of the globe is all one sea, and, truly seen, its tide is one."
– Ralph Waldo Emerson: *The Over-soul*

One
Cannot tell the difference between this interior and the world. All that is other breathes in here like an immanent wind. Walls are felled. An invisible hand takes and shakes like medicine. One is dispensed onto a random tongue, given to the ground as a libation.

I
You're an edible feast and could lose too much time. To avoid unwanted dissolving, you need to barricade yourself on all sides and post sentries. You may collapse even then, but at least there will be an ambulance.

119. a locked potential

The Other
"You will not easily find a man coming to grief through indifference to the workings of another's soul; but for those who pay no heed to the motions of their own, unhappiness is their sure reward."
– Marcus Aurelius: *Meditations*

One
The mind has made a prison of itself. Its bars are self-consciousness and fault-finding; its crimes are desire, doubt, envy and resentment. Its punitive device is isolation, which is accompanied by shame. The term has not been set.

I
If the shame is too shackling for prison-break or appeal, can't you scratch your questions on the walls, perform muscle-strengthening exercises, have a secret corner for an imagined picture of the outside? It's possible to make a life, even in here, and, who knows, some day the regime might be overthrown.

120. logocracy

The Other
"It is during the infant's so-called mirror phase, when it misrecognizes itself as Other, that the child accedes to language. This accession to language coincides with the primal repression of desire (union with the mother and displacements of desire), which then lingers on, embedded in the subject and his or her language."
– Ben Stoltzfus: *Lacan and Literature: Purloined Texts*

One
The body is grammaticised. Language rules it like a capricious dictator. There are constant interrogations, brutal reifyings, loud peremptory decrees. The words lodge like bricks, bind the muscles, weigh down the bones.

I
Sensitivity to language is my curse. A sentence can live in my head for years like an old bullet, poisoning the system. I try to control the voices, but as with horses, my hands must not leave the reins or they run wild. The best decisions are made in the quiet recesses between phrases.

121. sojourners

The Other
"The boy crouched in the room, rocking to and fro—like a beast in the Paris menagerie, the young doctor thought. He could not return his gaze, and his eyes wandered from one thing to the next, restlessly, insensibly. Sometimes a sudden spasm ran through the boy, a convulsive twitch that shook his whole body; but soon afterwards he would subside back into his habitual ceaseless motion. Locked in indifference, he submitted without affection to anyone who cared for him; he had bites and fierce scratches for those who thwarted his will."
– Michael Newton: *Savage Girls and Wild Boys*

One
Is self a dweller in the body or the body itself? One is given to spontaneous reactions, impulsive dance, inarticulate sounds, observation without intention.

I
The wild boy of Aveyron had awareness, but no language with which to construct and describe a sense of self. Without talk, life is unplotted, begins nowhere and leads to no conclusion. Or so it seems. Beneath our descriptions, the components of our physical system may have their own scenarios. In which case you, My Depth, and I, are both sojourners.

122. small bombs

The Other
"There is much in human affairs that can be accounted for at the level of the complex molecule. Who could ever reckon up the damage done to love and friendship and all hopes of happiness by a surfeit or depletion of this or that neuro-transmitter? And who will ever find a morality, an ethics down among the enzymes and amino acids when the general taste is for looking in the other direction?"
– Ian McEwan: *Saturday*

One
One is absorbed by the littler events, neuronal and social, that have ramifications and set profound puzzles. Politicians are not so real as these nano-spiders, fillips in the veins of action.

I
If the universe was once the size of a pea, then a moment can be a small bomb. To be there, sensing but also analysing, is surely to be a full human, fingertips on the soft trigger of the pulse.

123. judge and jury

The Other
"No law can be sacred to me but that of my nature."
– Ralph Waldo Emerson: *Self-reliance*

One
Repeatedly taking a scalpel to the moral tumour. It would be better to be impervious, an obsessed genius. But compassion and guilt spring up to crucify. Bleeding, then demon, then bleeding, then numb to dying.

I
You punish your perceived crimes with the assiduity of a torturer. Is this a programmed ethic, or the self-regulation of denial? Wielding your own whip, you're free from exposure and interference. But where's the legislation and who the jury? Justice, if it is yours, should be just.

124. amoral

The Other
"When all's said and done, the idea of the uniqueness of the individual is nothing more than pompous absurdity. We remember our own lives, Schopenhauer wrote somewhere, a little better than we do a novel we once read. That's about right: a little, no more."
– Michel Houellebecq: Spoken by the character, Michel, in *Platform*

One
In the way things happen, One sees process without purpose, a world that hoards or discards according to the whims of an incalculable dynamic. In this context, humans are as dispensable as trees and houseflies.

I
Others look to me for feelings tutored by morality and involvement. But I'm involved with the moral chasms between the seventy sextillion stars. I'm spun out, pointless, among the 125 million uncaring galaxies.

125. engaged

The Other
"I exist only as engaged."
– Jean-Paul Sartre: *Being and Nothingness*

One
The task is the thing. The stone is to be mined for the sake of the challenge itself, and to exercise One's talent for cutting and shaping. When the task is done well, there will be something to hold.

I
I can't assert with confidence that I know best. I have no large plan to benefit less talented, more ignorant beings. There's a desire for something to be done, and to be right, but nothing is quintessentially right, and obsessive focus renders me more separate with every success.

126. anachronism

The Other
"Life is first boredom, then fear.
Whether or not we use it, it goes,
And leaves what something hidden from us chose...."
– Philip Larkin: *Dockery and Son*

One
One is approached by others who see talent and want to be close. They want to produce in collaboration. But One shrinks and hugs One's knees, tongue-tied; reinforces the wall, as though One were jelly without it.

I
It's an age of communication and the collaborator. Books and papers are written by teams. The principle of egalitarianism, if not always practised, is common currency in the more prosperous parts of the world. It's no longer so easy to rest on one's laurels or make declarations without being challenged. This is a better way, but you hold me back.

127. a small view

The Other
"People wish to be settled; only as far as they are unsettled is there any hope for them."
– Ralph Waldo Emerson: *Selected Prose and Poetry*

One
Trapped within a small view, imprisoned by the round of routine and the work accepted as master. Forgetting, when the toes touch the floor each morning, that there are many other roads to walk.

I
It's easy for the loner to become obsessed with one or two aspects of life and push everything else to the side. But humanity develops by means of such obsessions. Knowledge is gained by people who ignore social and physical niceties in order to carry out exhaustive experiments, pore over study materials for endless hours, train themselves to the nth degree. With a small view, you might at least have direction.

128. pitch

The Other
"No one who survives to speak
new language, has avoided this:
the cutting-away of an old force that held her
rooted to an old ground
the pitch of utter loneliness
where she herself and all creation
seem equally dispersed, weightless, her being a cry
to which no echo comes or can ever come."
– Adrienne Rich: *Transcendental Etude*

One
On the upper deck of a bus, looking out the window. The
passengers might as well be holograms. Contact is impossible.
Whatever happens, One will have no part to play. There are
shapes, but none makes sense.

I
I try to contain a fierce sorrow within my quaking frame.
This is a desperate moment. It may also be the moment
when I draw close to the border of wisdom, or so I tell
myself, repeating something I once read. Life's content is
largely the product of one's verdict upon it. It might feel as
though I'm hovering in space, but space has potential too.
This thought will fade when it finishes its sentence.

129. who's home?

The Other
"The unavoidable conclusion seems to be that when the individual faces torture or annihilation, he cannot rely on the resources of his own individuality. His only source of strength is in not being himself but part of something mighty, glorious and indestructible. Faith here is primarily a process of identification; the process by which the individual ceases to be himself and becomes part of something eternal."
– Eric Hoffer: *The True Believer*

One
One is obsessively protective of this separate unit, but even so, to lose One's self seems a beautiful prospect.

I
Is it cowardice that generates thoughts of oblivion? Is transcendence another word for desertion? If so, is that such a crime? If you believe that the soldiers will shortly break down the door, it seems rational to make sure you're not in.

mirror

130. fashion or fault

The Other
"I exist as I am, that is enough,
If no other in the world be aware I sit content,
And if each and all be aware I sit content."
– Walt Whitman: *Leaves of Grass*

One
One attends to detail in dress as in everything else, as though living were performance. One is focused by fashion. Compulsively, One searches for the right look, the quirky accessory, lives in these concerns as in fantasy. One is not enough in Oneself.

I
You dreamt of a horse running through water, looking neither right nor left, splashing indiscriminately. Its eyes were wild, self-approving. Could that be you? All that's natural has spontaneous expression. Splash and be redeemed.

131. sartorial rites

The Other
"The man of the world almost always wears a mask."
– Jean-Jacques Rousseau: *Émile*

One
Recurring dreams of wardrobes packed with clothes.
Bewildered among the hangers, racked with choice. Body is
worn with a difference each time. No fixed mode.

I
The benefit of ritual is said to be contained in the process
itself, the effect produced *'ex opere operato'*—'from the work
done'. I perform ritual when I dress, though the form isn't a
given. If my mood changes day by day, it's only appropriate
that my outer appearance should, bravely, correspond.

132. reflective instrument

The Other
"Dr. Montessori said, 'the child takes in his whole environment, not with his mind but with his life'."
– Maria Montessori: *http://www.montessorisv.com/maria-montessori.htm*

One
One is the world's best reflector. Here are the others in 3D. One is a recording instrument, playing them back at random, performing without even trying.

I
I hear others when I speak, feel them when I move. Only when alone does my state approach stability, but not quite, because humans are not the only entities that affect.

133. imitation of life

The Other
"Life is painful and disappointing. It is useless, therefore, to write new realistic novels. We generally know where we stand in relation to reality and don't care to know any more. Humanity, such as it is, inspires only an attenuated curiosity in us."
– Michel Houellebecq: *H.P. Lovecraft Against the World, Against Life*

One
One tries to improve One's condition by mimicking how others live. Sit and play games, shop at new stores, discuss politics and popular topics. Always there is lack, a desire for deeper communion.

I
Imitation is how humans become. But why do you so often mimic the uninspired? There are people worthy of emulation. It's acceptable to adopt a role model and, for you, maybe it's necessary.

134. invasions

The Other
"Everything I do is some kind of modified borrowing from others who have been close to me either actually or virtually, and the virtual influences are among the most profound."
– Douglas Hofstadter: *I am a Strange Loop*

One
Fearful from the first. Prods would come from the circumambience, probing the quiet jelly of consciousness. One would protest, but with the skin and pulse only. Foreigners entered and stayed, interfered with the environment, stole the singular stance, induced confusion. Which endures.

I
Where would you set your boundary? A metre beyond the epidermis? A centimetre? At the walls of the blood vessels? Every organism is porous, with to-and-fro traffic. In such territory, who's the foreigner?

135. float or fall

The Other
"Just imagine a life without mirrors. You'd dream about your face and imagine it as an outer reflection of what is inside you."
– Milan Kundera: *Immortality*

One
The observations of others fix One in space and time, imprison. One wants to be undefined, not residing anywhere in particular, free to be stone or feather.

I
Where political liberty prevails, the greatest freedom we can reach is from society's notions of achievement and the castigating search for conclusions. These chains are internalised and can be broken by thought. The only factor stopping us from behaving as we wish is fear of the responsibility.

136. disassociated

The Other
"But essentially I desired solitude and independence: not in the English form of quiet home life in the country, but rather after the fashion of ancient philosophers, often in exile, but always in sight of the market-place and the theatre."
– George Santayana: *My Host the World*

One
It is easiest to be with people when there is a task to be done. One is inept in the casual sharing of mundane detail, being either uncertain of Oneself or bored with the quotidian. At One's best when dealing with others on an official basis, because the rules of relationship are clear and agreed. Simple fellow-feeling is a challenge that finds One retreating to the back-room with iPod, book and laptop.

I
People who veer towards Asperger's syndrome often value efficiency more than ideology. Obsession with detail reduces the capacity for flow that social intercourse demands.

137. fermion or boson

The Other

"It is because fermions can't get into the same state (share identities) that matter can be solid. Matter depends on their unsociability. On the other hand, it is because bosons can get into the same state that we have large-scale waves and forces. But there is no sharp cutoff point and in the right circumstances even the most determinedly individualistic fermion can be drawn into a deeper relationship. No recluse is entirely safe from the temptations of society. In fact this tension between particles and waves at the quantum level does seem to mirror in an interesting way the similar tension between individuals and groups in human society."
– Danah Zohar: *The Quantum Self*

One

You are so certain of who you are, person-with-community. You care; you are a fountain of sweet emotion; you have a heart. The heart in here is an organ pumping blood.

I

Beneath the social niceties there's other work in progress— the calculating machinations of politics, the precision of the intellectual; you could say the reptilian life of the fermion. Those focused on the social glue think emotion is the reality, but species survival is always an issue. Social ties improve survival odds. Emotions are survival responses to which people give pretty names. There's nothing wrong with any of this, and no need to imagine a higher motive, unless I want to ease my anxiety. You, My Depth, are my unease—a fermion with a boson desire.

138. contradictions

The Other
"... uncontradicting solitude
Supports me on its giant palm...."
– Philip Larkin: *Best Society*

One
When others are absent, One must pretend they do not exist.
It is impossible to feel all those lives and also be One's self.

I
Those who experience your distance would find it hard to believe how deeply they affect you. The depth is what arrests—an emotional maze, bedevilled by misdirection.

139. unemployed

The Other

"The subjective can be so over-emphasized that the individual's inner world becomes entirely divorced from reality. In that case we call him mad. On the other hand, as Winnicott points out, the individual can suppress his inner world in such a way that he becomes over-compliant with external reality. If the individual regards the external world merely as something to which he has to adapt, rather than as something in which his subjectivity can find fulfilment, his individuality disappears and his life becomes meaningless or futile."

– Anthony Storr: *Solitude*

One

When it appears that One is about to belong to an occupation or profession, One draws back. The assumption of an epithet, however praiseworthy, savours of loss. After the podium, One sees a high table and an incontrovertible way to hold a knife and fork.

I

Before I'm a teacher, writer, carpenter, electrician, I'm a collection of physical and intellectual faculties. Functioning in commercial structures demands the translation of these into an occupation. You, however, are unemployable.

140. objective

The Other

"The only 'momentum' that accrues to the trajectory of a self, or a club, is the stability imparted to it by the web of beliefs that constitute it, and when those beliefs lapse, it lapses, either permanently or temporarily."
– Daniel Dennett: *Consciousness Explained*

One

How to form opinions when so often the feelings do not give rise to them? How to react to events? What are the measures of joy and tragedy? Things patently revolting to others can leave One unmoved. One is considered cold.

I

Objectivity is being outlawed in popular discourse and casual social encounters, but it's still the cornerstone of scholarship and the foundation of good judgement. We should nurture it, not deny it for the sake of proving that we feel.

141. pretender

The Other
"Playing at goodness, like going to church?"
– Philip Larkin: *Vers de Société*

One
Seething, twisting with pent-up desire. Want to shatter polite structures, become scaly in the cave, make forays for loot. All this beneath the gentle façade of a liar.

I
I'm learning to pretend. It appears that lying is necessary for social harmony. Sometimes, under the radar, you become so still that I'm afraid you're plotting.

142. code

The Other
"They can't let on I'm there. There's nothing down on paper.
  What there is is code.
Alone? I'm sometimes. Very. Very. Sometimes very hot and
  sometimes very cold."
– Ciaran Carson: *Two to Tango*

One
Impatient with the careful social intuiting that seems
required. Why do they use code? Why do they not express
themselves directly and make the route to understanding
less labyrinthine? The multitude of possibilities precludes
even a starting point.

I
Everything apperceived is in one language or another. You
receive the messages you seek, see what you're programmed
to see, apprehend the objects of your attention. The brain is
constantly decoding. You might consider abdicating your
supreme purity and learning the languages of others. It's not
imperative that yours be the mother tongue.

143. *sic semper tyrannis*

The Other
"I came into this world, not chiefly to make this a good place to live in, but to live in it, good or bad."
– Henry David Thoreau: *Civil Disobedience*

One
Antagonistic, currying anger, always in search of engagement. Must live in extreme expression of the whole self.

I
And so in opposition to show your strength. And so to show your weakness. Can you not be passionate, competitive, industrious? If you can't remove the need to challenge others, can you bear the alienation it invites? An extreme self creates a vacuum with its fierce spin.

144. native

The Other
"For masterpieces are not single and solitary births: they are the outcome of many years of thinking in common, of thinking by the body of the people, so that the experience of the mass is behind the single voice."
– Virginia Woolf: *A Room of One's Own*

One
How involved is One in the political unit? What does it mean when 'England goes to war', 'Germany likes Canada', 'Iran has nuclear weapons'? When 'Ireland' wins a football match, how deeply is One implicated, when One is not the immediate agent and has many other aspects apart from racial identity? There are too many differences between compatriots to resolve them by synecdoche.

I
By coming to life within its borders, we share in the actions and achievements of others in the nation state. There's a common genetic inheritance and a shared environmental constitution. Even so, it's possible to identify deeply with a nation other than my own, or with none. There are more bacteria in the mouth than there are people in New York city; I'm native to an infinitely large universe, and a nation unto myself.

145. mould

The Other
"What Montaigne discovered in himself—as others could in their own case too—was a self which was governed by a 'forme maistresse', a 'mastermould' which effectively resisted any attempt to change it by education or indoctrination."
– M. A. Screech: Introduction to *Michel de Montaigne, The Complete Essays*

One
One is not tuned, lacks the acceptable style, whether of empathy, sympathy, dispute or adulation. If only One could assume an effective personality—be orderly, pleasant and self-protective.

I
The ideal personality is a metaphorical expression of qualities and propensities. Most people produce one with the minimum of thought. I labour on mine, mould by mould.

146. interesting perversity

The Other

"The natural man lives for himself; he is the unit, the whole, dependent only on himself and on his like. The citizen is but the numerator of a fraction, whose value depends on its denominator; his value depends upon the whole, that is, on the community."

– Jean-Jacques Rousseau: *Émile*

One

Everybody sees this hostility to the norm. One is trying to reach out, they should believe that. One is not malicious. But when something is said as if it were definitive, One rebels and asserts the opposite. Because why should this thing be so and that not? One is perverse.

I

If I learned diplomacy and knew how to say the acceptable things while keeping my own counsel, would my life be any better? Would social acceptance be sufficient consolation for the loss of an interesting perversity?

147. perfidy

The Other
"When past trauma has eroded the efficiency of the brainstem's vagal brake, the resulting propensity to fight, flight or freezing is almost always maladaptive."
– David J. Wallin: *Attachment in Psychotherapy*

One
The stomach buckles. Can't stop the shaking inside, from the underside of the skin to deep within the organs. It is an other's success, an other who cares. Because they have moved close, there is an impulse to gnaw. One takes regular counts: of their words, their talents, their failings, their friends, their every free impulse. However much they reassure, they seem perfidious. Their joy causes pain, and the impulse to destroy possesses the wits, sends One into a headlong rampage.

I
You're unbearable. You must be destroyed. There's nothing for you to achieve in this world. What does it matter if you die now rather than another time? Let me take you to the ocean. The wide compulsive ocean. Or the swollen river. Or the rope, yes, the slow-devouring rope. All the better to make you suffer.

148. a dog's life

The Other

"I have never believed that man's freedom consisted in doing what he wants, but rather in never doing what he does not want to do...."

– Jean-Jacques Rousseau: *The Reveries of the Solitary Walker*

One

Why dress? Why wash? The wild world never washes except when forced by rain. One wants to be naked but hidden, like all those creatures that disgust when the rock is turned over.

I

The cynics were accused of living like dogs (hence their name, from the Greek *kynikos*, literally 'dog-like'). A group of artists in sixteenth-century Florence were also said to live like brute beasts, never washing hands, faces or beards. They didn't sweep their houses and only made their beds every two months; they drank from bottles or jugs. How many teenagers live just like this? If it occurs spontaneously, if it comforts to be careless, so be it.

149. *modus vivendi*

The Other
"A culture could be defined, from one point of view, as a system of standards of what counts as intelligible reasons for acting."
– Eric Matthews: *Mind: Key Concepts in Philosophy*

One
Could become like one of those miserable loners in city bedsits who fry everything and eat out of the pan, rustics far from their cosseting mothers. What's the point in table manners and parlour behaviours? Such transitory expressions of One's existence are meaningless.

I
Nothing has inherent meaning; there are only causes and motivations. Style in living is symbolic. Adopting the current *modus vivendi* shows willingness to participate at some level of the social process, profers the hand of co-operation and tolerance. Discipline may also bring personal benefits. Certainly, there are benefits in cleanliness and good eating, not to mention the personal enhancement of a beautiful environment. It's often its pragmatic value that keeps a custom alive.

150. sublimation

The Other
"Beyond all this, the wish to be alone:
However the sky grows dark with invitation-cards...."
– Philip Larkin: *Wants*

One
Will not come out. Polishing again and again the beloved internal effects. And then, on examination, there hardly seems to be anything here of value, relative to the glitter in the windows of others.

I
The mystics call their desire for solitude a wish to be closer to God, who, in the absence of proof to the contrary, must be located in their own psyches. Thomas Merton postulated that in contemplating this location they change the consciousness of others by means of the 'sublime fire of infused love'. It's mooted in scientific circles that the human organism can't be isolated at a sub-atomic level. So maybe we're sharing whether we like it or not. If we listen to music in the solitude of our home, give ourselves sexual pleasure, study, consider the principles of phenomena, sit reading by our sublimating gas fire, might we be infusing self-love into the universal consciousness?

151. available

The Other

> "In solitude
> What happiness, who can enjoy alone,
> Or all enjoying, what contentment find?"
> – John Milton: *Paradise Lost*

One

One is eminently available. Doing nothing most nights. Or the same old things. Why don't they come? Life is not a progression but a shuttling back and forth between fixed states, moidered.

I

I must create each day by and for myself. There are others who might be companions, but I must first be my own. This does not feel just. How do you begin without a starting point?

152. selfless

The Other

"There is no whole self. Any of life's present situations is seamless and sufficient. Are you, as you ponder these disquietudes, anything more than an indifference gliding over the argument I make, or an appraisal of the opinions I expound?

I, as I write this, am only a certainty that seeks out the words that are most apt to compel your attention. That proposition and a few muscular sensations, and the sight of the limpid branches that the trees place outside my window, constitute my current I."

– Jorge Luis Borges: *The Nothingness of Personality*

One

Must One declare an identity? *One likes this, does not like that; One is a teacher, a plumber, a soldier, right-wing, left-wing....* What if One has no preferences, cannot pinpoint abiding needs, fails to cohere in definition?

I

There may be nothing in here but fragmented phenomena in the universe of the body and the body's bodies. This is anarchy, with no possibility of a centre. I can't be my own harbour, can only be a sailor forever on the high seas. I brace myself, afraid I might veer into chaos, when already in its vicinity, knowing the pull of its breath.

153. simulation

The Other
"Instinctively, he had already become proficient in the habit of simulating that he was someone, so that others would not discover his condition as no one...."
– Jorge Luis Borges: *Everything and Nothing*

One
One tries on a voice and a new way of walking. They stare. They do not believe. They are right, of course. One does not live in these acts as they do.

I
On its own, an audio loop makes no sound. It needs a non-null input. It's the same with the self: input determines output. I learn language and behaviour from others; they're expressed in the context of others, whether by means of books, audio-visual media or physical presence. In the loner, much remains unsounded.

154. borg

The Other
"But I felt: you are an *I*,
You are an *Elizabeth*,
you are one of *them*."
– Elizabeth Bishop: *In the Waiting Room*

One
To utter a pronoun seems a large act. Why is *I* not *you*, *he* or *she*? When is *we* not *they*? One does not want to be simply an other. Nor pinpointed to impalement.

I
The personal pronoun fails on my lips, conscious of its lack of referent, like a currency without value. Although I may seem thoroughly reinforced, isolation often feels like the only way I can avoid assimilation.

155. collage

The Other
"We are all curious collages, weird little planetoids that grow by accreting other people's habits and ideas and styles and tics and jokes and phrases and tunes and hopes and fears as if they were meteorites that came soaring out of the blue, collided with us, and stuck."
– Douglas Hofstadter: *I am a Strange Loop*

One
No way of knowing which feelings start here and which are echoes from beyond. Others' needs and thoughts become One's own. In conflict, One is never sure who or what started it.

I
Permeability can either cause madness or maintain sanity, depending on its colour and tone. It's truest to say that we're all part of an immense dynamic, where the ultimate cause, therefore the subsidiary ones, are forever in doubt.

156. masquerade

The Other
"It was the mask engaged your mind,
And after set your heart to beat,
Not what's behind."
– W. B. Yeats: *The Mask*

One
A masquerade. *Look, I wear this, it's what I am; I do this, it's what I am; I've achieved this, it's what I am.* The masks are relentless interrogators: *And who? And why?* One labours to answer, morning, noon and night. Especially at night, when they appear stark against the backdrop. They are the real ghosts.

I
If our masks were to melt, what would there be to see? We wear our body as we wear our clothes. Every phenomenon is the expression of a substance or order we could not otherwise intuit. Strip off the skin, pound the bones, mince the organs, and there would remain some ungraspable entity, eloping with its microscopic lover into the weave of the cosmic veil.

157. lamb

The Other
"People who see their lives as irremediably spoiled cannot find a worth-while purpose in self-advancement.... Anything undertaken under the auspices of the self seem to them foredoomed. Nothing that has its roots and reasons in the self can be good and noble."
– Eric Hoffer: *The True Believer*

One
One gives Oneself to the cause, the work, the person in need. Striking for Oneself makes no sense. What cannot be done without? How can One rise when others languish? One asks for nothing.

I
I sacrifice and later see others overtake me in personal satisfaction. Am I really disposable, or do I deny my needs in order to assert moral superiority? There's nobody who accepts life and doesn't self-nurture.

158. joy, the usurper

The Other
"If for one moment I were to lose my grip on the world, it would fall apart...."
– J. M. Coetzee: *In the Heart of the Country*

One
They smile and ask how One is. Why does One reply with talk of the tainted wine? Must One always be embroiled in difficulty? It feels like abdication to admit joy.

I
Walking in a desert you can hope for an oasis, but you can't fill each moment with the hope or you bind yourself to the fickle future. And if you arrive to the heart of fertility you might still not laugh, because for so long your desires have been particulate in space, unmiraged by the kindred face of an other.

159. glister

The Other
"... Why I have persevered to shun
The common paths that others run;
And on a strange road journeyed on
Heedless alike of Wealth and Power —
Of Glory's wreath and Pleasure's flower."
– Emily Jane Brontë: *'Oh, thy bright eyes must answer now'*

One
Others fill their lives with things and the hope of things. Their houses matter, their possessions matter. One's diffused centre struggles to find any practice or collection that might be valuable.

I
The only ultimate goal appears to be survival. All efforts can be traced back to it, one way or another. Reading this sub-text, I'm paralysed and can't construct a hierarchy of value. I might move towards what's shiny if only I could stop looking back for a supportive face.

160. unaccomplished

The Other
"But if I am in an unfamiliar place, among a number of strange people, or people whom I feel to be strangers, the whole room presses on my chest and I am unable to move, my whole personality seems virtually to get under their skins, and everything becomes hopeless."
– Franz Kafka: *Letters to Felice*

One
As though this were the first utterance. The intention is slow to be brought to speech and does not sound quite right. Accompanied by the effects of a flushed face and stutterings, the performance is a deal short of accomplished.

I
There's need to be nervous, because life is a performance and others might deride, or worse, disregard you. You must be in possession of yourself. Prepare, becalm, take your time. Indulge an element of secrecy.

161. approver

The Other

"... that the savage lives within himself while social man lives constantly outside himself, and only knows how to live in the opinion of others, so that he seems to receive the consciousness of his own existence merely from the judgement of others concerning him."

– Jean-Jacques Rousseau: *A Discourse on the Origin and Foundation of the Inequality of Mankind*

One

One rarely has a thought that doesn't imagine an audience. One argues the case to the fictive others and pre-runs their yeas and nays as though they had a share in all that occurs.

I

The child very early becomes displaced, because it can't live both in itself and in society. It's doubly displaced if there's an absence of reinforcing contact. We must learn to be our own interlaced fingers, our own reassuring embrace, and more importantly, our own rational arbiter. After all, it's I who must live this life.

162. pretty pictures

The Other
"There are emotions that seek to kill the solitary; if they do not succeed, well, they must die themselves! But are you capable of being a murderer?"
– Friedrich Nietzsche: *Thus Spake Zarathustra*

One
Long after the other has left, his face breaks back in. One cannot be subject to the arbitrary behaviour of a projection. One must not depend, for fear of becoming slave.

I
In lone times it's normal to create imaginary others. It bolsters our humanity. Monks and mystics posit an immanent presence which they experience as a relationship; non-religious loners may be obsessed with achievers in sport, science or the arts. For most people there's a relative or mentor who acts as a support in absentia. Without a redeeming image, memories turn monster in the cramped prison you make of yourself.

163. garbled messages

The Other
"... when I am with other people I find it nearly impossible not to be aware of them, and that awareness breaks up the silence. I worry occasionally that this may have something to do with the thinness of my sense of self, which can be so easily overwhelmed by others...."
– Sara Maitland: *The Book of Silence*

One
There is little awareness of all those others who pass by on an everyday street. But when they address One, their voices burst in over-amplified and cannot be blocked. A harsh voice penetrates the skin and twists the stomach; a contrived, insidious tone disables; one strong and clear convinces of any cause.

I
The vehicle is not the thing itself. Humans and their speech are consummate dissemblers, for the sake of both self-protection and sensitivity. The tone you hear might not be that intended. You spontaneously respond and I misinterpret.

164. ruminant

The Other
"What kind of a support are illusions which delude me alone in the whole world? The whole present generation sees only errors and prejudices in the sentiments with which I alone nourish myself."

– Jean-Jacques Rousseau: *The Reveries of the Solitary Walker*

One
Others settle truths in a few facile phrases. One tends to chew a question for years, made swollen and immobile by its endless permutations.

I
I expect every conversation to be satisfying, even transformative. I expect my thoughts to establish, if not conclusions, at least definite direction. I expect my moments to have meat. Should I change my company, my methods or my expectations?

165. cells

The Other
"Trust thyself: every heart vibrates to that iron string. Accept the place the divine providence has found for you, the society of your contemporaries, the connection of events."
– Ralph Waldo Emerson: *Self-Reliance*

One
Others are bewildering and contradictory. Their faces hide their lives; their talk belies their motives and inclinations. Friends barely know each other's minds. Where is the communing they boast of?

I
Unity and separateness are less complex ideas for others. For them, there's no paradox in being both self-sealed and part of a group. This is, after all, the nature of those basic building blocks, the cells.

166. hounded

The Other
"The eremitic life means reconciling the impulses and instincts of aggression, anger, lust, and pride with the spiritual values of renunciation, disengagement, humility, and non-possession."
– Meng-hu: *http://www.hermitary.com/articles/flue.html*

One
One grows weary of pressure from outside. Eyes in hot pursuit, questions with growling interdicts at their heels. Snap like a hounded fox.

I
It's a mistake to presume either hostility or friendship. I must be calm, accept the various aspects of my life without ascribing value, assess my needs and those of others, act with circumspection. If necessary, snap.

167. common sensibility

The Other
"Conversation takes the importance, the seriousness, the truth out of everything I think."
– Franz Kafka: *Kafka Diaries 1910–1913*

One
During the interval, the woman in the next seat turns and asks with an intimate tone if One is enjoying the play. One barely suppresses an insult. The play is stunning, magnificent, has sliced One into several barely strung pieces. One wants to retort, *Shut your mouth and open your feelings.*

I
They expect you to reduce yourself to a common sensibility. They are trying, I know, to connect. It's human. They might even want to learn, to expand their understanding and include you in their ambit. But entry to the inner chamber is only for the initiate.

168. tsunami

The Other
"Most critical of all, perhaps, is the extent to which our early attachments have (or have not) provided us with the relational experience of a secure base, and, thus, the foundation for a mental representation of an *internalized* secure base."
– David J. Wallin: *Attachment in Psychotherapy*

One
Every so often, an other reaches across the divide and the touch is intimate. Doors fly open, letting in wind and water. Possessions are flooded or carried away. Nothing about One can be confirmed.

I
This is the usurpation you wished for. Be it inspiration, love or delusion, you may emerge enriched. Cling until the waters recede.

169. idol of the heart

The Other
"I began to fear that, in making friendship the idol of my heart, I had wasted my life in sacrificing to chimeras."
– Jean-Jacques Rousseau: *The Confessions*

One
Yes, One is sometimes touched by an other, but the closeness of two bodies is still only a far connection, like the remote signal between a beetle and a single helium atom of the sun.

I
I hope for complete union, for the lover to pass through my skin and turn my insides into a shared home. But the mix is never quite right. Love is the loner's Everest. It's not clear what I should aim for and what I should consider enough.

170. bell

The Other
"While I saw a thousand conspiracies formed around me, all I could complain of was the tyranny of those whom I called my friends, and whose only object, as I imagined, was to force me to be happy in their own fashion rather than in my own."
– Jean-Jacques Rousseau: *The Confessions*

One
One listens exhaustively to the views and needs of an other. One is absorbed and forgets One's own life. Everything external seems more valid and urgent. One is empty as a silver bell.

I
I offer my services and think it friendship, but I don't know how to give and retain in equal measure. I become depleted. Resentfully reclaim the lot.

171. placate or avoid

The Other
"The child who has not, in infancy, formed secure bonds of trust with attachment figures, may react to parents, and later to other people, in a variety of ways; but I suggest that these variants are founded upon two basic themes. The first is *placation*; the second, *avoidance*. I shall try to show that placation is associated with the development of a depressive personality whilst avoidance is associated with the development of a schizoid personality."
– Anthony Storr: *Solitude*

One
One wishes to be perfect and, if criticised, creeps away like an injured child. If there is no disturbance from outside, One draws on the inner stock of plaints, buckles at disappointments, counts and recounts the flaws, chews nails as far as they will go.

I
I'm not valued for my indefinable self, but for what I do and give. Relationships are conditional transactions. The fact that I can't always perform to the highest standards is a good enough reason to be alone. I may, of course, be wrong in presuming that if others aren't indulged, they'll disparage, despise and depart.

172. uncoupled

The Other

"The burden of value with which we are at present loading interpersonal relationships is too heavy for those fragile craft to carry. Our expectation that satisfying intimate relationships should, ideally, provide happiness and that, if they do not, there must be something wrong with these relationships, seems to be exaggerated."
– Anthony Storr: *Solitude*

One

Living with somebody is to expose Oneself to daily censure. It is a rare other who does not demand. One's life becomes flooded with scrutinising light. And then, despite all the interference, they expect One to know One's own way and withstand their periodic withdrawals.

I

You lie. I can see that others are happy in their coupled state. There are people who accept each other with all their variegations. I've met nobody who says it's simple, many who think it's better than being alone. You describe yourself when you speak of demands and withdrawals.

173. home alone

The Other
"A novel way to think about depression ... is that lowered serotonin levels in the brain lead to distorted decision making in social situations, which may trigger feelings of alienation."
– Laura Spinney: *New Scientist* magazine

One
Going home alone, with that challenging look still mid-way between the nipples like a probe, trying to fix One's position on the map. One makes sure to detach from the beam, then topples off the edge of the world, fully clothed, nothing becoming.

I
It's remarkably difficult to find the right conditions for love or something resembling it. I might be constitutionally resistant. There's nothing to be done, at least tonight. I could perhaps exploit the backwash of alcohol and enlarge what slight suggestions there have been; let the brain interpret the hand's thrust as love.

174. loss

The Other
"'If a man, sunk in deep sleep, rests dreamlessly, this is the Self, the Immortal, the Assured, the Universal Being.'

'In such a condition, O Exalted One, a man does not know of his Self that 'This is I', and that 'these are beings'. He is gone to annihilation. I see nothing propitious here.'

'That,' replies Prajapati, 'is indeed so.'"
– From the *Upanishads*, quoted in Martin Buber: *I and Thou*

One
One does not fear death, which is only the loss of awareness. One greatly fears the loss of approval, the loss of physical contact, the loss of purpose, the pure, unworried, bright silence; the awareness of all that loss here and now.

I
Thich Nhat Hanh named the three doors of liberation as Emptiness, Signlessness and Aimlessness. You're intimately acquainted with them all. Feel free.

175. safe love

The Other
"Self-preservation requires, therefore, that we shall love ourselves; we must love ourselves above everything, and it follows directly from this that we love what contributes to our preservation."
– Jean-Jacques Rousseau: *Émile*

One
When nightmares come and a spectre grasps the hand, claiming a vessel for embodiment, One longs for an other in the bed to scatter the terrors. But One cannot simply acquire a protector. One must surely be brave enough to seek a true feeling and desire the other only for their inherent beauty.

I
Love is often about self-preservation. People rest more easily when accompanied and supported. The phrase 'together for life' assumes a new meaning in this light. I've believed that love should be unconditional, not posited on performance, but have proved unequal to the ideal. Nor, now that I look, do I see others so noble.

176. market

The Other
"I have my own stern claims and perfect circle. It denies the name of duty to many offices that are called duties."
– Ralph Waldo Emerson: *Self-reliance*

One
How to trade without a sense of worth? One wants a price tag. Is it ever safe to trust a declaration of love when lovability cannot be proved? One wilts in the relational marketplace.

I
Who or what is the arbiter of worth? Begin with this: the fact that you're here means the natural world has sanctioned your existence. You're a phenomenon like a plant or wild animal, with the same existential rationale. The next move is yours.

inaccurate map

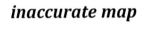

177. what nature willed

The Other
"These hours of solitude and meditation are the only ones in the day during which I am fully myself and for myself, without diversion, without obstacle, and during which I can truly claim to be what nature willed."
– Jean-Jacques Rousseau: *The Reveries of the Solitary Walker*

One
Why does the body not express the meaning inside? It restricts itself to social mannerisms, trains the voice in submission to that banal choir where everyone sings the same phrase in endless repetition. It will not dance the prime dance. It is a dissembler—worse—a traitor.

I
How can one expression of the individual be 'what nature willed', and another not? The pre-frontal cortex, though the latest part of the brain to develop, is no less the brain than the cerebellum. The civilising thrust of the forebrain is as natural, because biologically motivated, as the animal instinct of the brainstem. There's no traitor here; just dialogue or argument, and sometimes, prolonged war.

178. craving

The Other

"Men wrongly complain of Experience; with great abuse they accuse her of leading them astray but they set Experience aside, turning from it with complaints as to our ignorance causing us to be carried away by vain and foolish desires to promise ourselves, in her name, things that are not in her power; saying that she is fallacious."
– Leonardo da Vinci: *The Notebooks of Leonardo da Vinci 1*

One

One spends each day thinking of the next. The pivots? That morning latté, the fruit pastry, the bag of tortilla chips, the chocolate. One craves too the mind-altering bottles of wine, the spliff, those incidental lovers that always leave One wanting more.

I

There's a two-pronged approach to control of cravings: one is to consider the consequences of their satisfaction; the other is to fill the body with something else.

179. sloth

The Other
"Our sixth combat is with what the Greeks call *accedia*, which we may term spiritual weariness or distress of heart. This is akin to dejection, and is especially trying to solitaires, and a dangerous and common enemy to dwellers of the desert; and especially disturbing to a monk about the sixth hour (midday), like some fever which seizes him at stated times, bringing the burning heat of its attacks on the sick man at usual and regular hours. Lastly, there are some of the elders who declare that this is the 'noonday demon' spoken of in the ninetieth Psalm."
– St. John Cassian: *The Training of a Monk and the Eight Deadly Sins*

One
One circles tasks as a predator might circle a target, but not with a predator's focus. One's effort is a spatter of rain against the window of a speeding car. Is it a craving for company that makes One get busy instead with desultory pottering and random chewing? The senses are not engaged and the day topples into oblivion.

I
The lone life is sustained by commitment to task and method. Failure in this can lead to disturbance, as might flaws in the day's choreography. Monasteries have a system of offices to programme the hours. As generator of my own routine, I might learn from the monks and create a diurnal map.

180. blink

The Other

"... as I look backward upon my own writing, I take pleasure alone in those verses where it seems to me I have found something hard and cold, some articulation of the Image which is the opposite of all that I am in my daily life, and all that my country is; yet man or nation can no more make this Mask or Image than the seed can be made by the soil into which it is cast."

– W. B. Yeats: *The Autobiography of William Butler Yeats*

One

One imagines: walking into a room where everyone knows One's name; a coterie of laughing friends in the buzzing bar of a hotel; arms around One in a deep-mattressed bed. When these are realities, One swells with importance, becomes intoxicated, gabbles and misbehaves, then blinks and is back in the familiar empty chamber.

I

My astrological chart displays the problem: Saturn in the seventh house. Others are the structure-makers of my life and relationships are difficult, perhaps even oppressive. No amount of expert pretence or acquired expertise will kill what is natural to the organism. Believe or not.

181. name

The Other
"Whoever degrades another degrades me ... and whatever is
    done or said at last returns to me,
And whatever I do or say I also return."
– Walt Whitman: *Leaves of Grass*

One
One casts for a name and finds a shallow pool. Deeper, by
billions of years, is namelessness. What label can tell a
history? One's name—breath out in any tone and you'll find
it.

I
If your name is every sound on the wind, how are you to be
distinguished from the wind? Is that the old poetic assertion
that we are in everything and everything is in us? This
notion is fundamental to many philosophies and seems
correct to me, but a person is a distinct, if tiny, event within
the dynamic. DNA is a thread of individuality that defines us,
but will not do in introductions. For the want of something
more accurate, I can only say, 'I', and let you move as you
will.

182. *mundus internus*

The Other
"It seems to me more than ever that I am a victim of introspection. If I have not the power to put myself in the place of other people, but must be continually burrowing inward, I shall never be the magnanimous creative person I wish to be. Yet I am hypnotized by the workings of the individual, alone, and am continually using myself as a specimen."
– Sylvia Plath: *The Unabridged Journals of Sylvia Plath*

One
This body is a sensing mechanism, but it is so engaged with itself that its phenomena make a hinterland of the planet.

I
Humans are so self-aware that they're well beyond the state of just being. So, sensing isn't enough; we must study—inner and outer phenomena, interpretations, experiments, philosophies. We're a biological unit on another biological unit, the planet, so learning of our hinterland is learning of ourselves. *Mundus internus* equals *unus mundus*.

183. buffeted

The Other
"Solitude would have crushed her had she not fallen into hermit skills and become one more thing that moved in the natural world."
– Toni Morrison: *A Mercy*

One
Daytime sounds are huge—the rumble of traffic, wayward sirens, café chatter, electrical hums. Have learned to shut many of them out, but the vibrations still do their work, and it's no longer clear what it is that sends the skin into a tremble.

I
The skin may tremble, the organs may convulse, you may clamour for escape, for satisfaction; but I must remain calm, like a teacher with an awkward pupil. I don't want to play that role. I want to be the protected child.

184. rabid

The Other
"A want of friends points to envy or arrogance."
– Friedrich Nietzsche: *Human all Too Human*

One
Distrustful wild dog—hoarding bones, snatching pieces of meat from passers-by. One's own needs prevail over all other concerns. What are the troubles of society to the indigent? One's allegiance is to the hungry self, that monster.

I
If you weren't so rabid, I could perhaps hide your social flaws. But you rush the floodgates and pour out undirected. The only recourse is to become sequestered, focus on some engaging work, try not to become so manic that I make myself ill.

185. savant

The Other
"... usque adeone scire tuum nihil est, nisi te scire hoc sciat alter?"

"... is all that you know worthless to you unless another knows that you know it?"
– Persius: *Satires*

One
Knowledge, but no other's ear to receive it. Not sure where to send or what kind of language could transmit. One learns lonely, without agreement or dispute.

I
Why do you need to speak when your knowledge can be worked into daily actions? I should tend my intellect untroubled, make my own assessments, set my own programme. I can't measure the benefits of my knowledge for others, but I can savour its every edification in myself.

186. antiphon

The Other
"What can a book give us that a relationship can't? One possible answer might be 'the experience of a relationship in silence'—the unusual experience of a relationship in which no one speaks. Our present interest in biography, in knowing about writers is, I think, a wish to break this silence."
– Adam Phillips: *Promises, Promises*

One
Ears primed for the antiphon. A tone comes close but is distorted by a host of stimuli. Withdraw. Find in the written word or recorded music a clear, unbrokered note, to which One can respond without fear of disruption.

I
The body intervenes between one reaching mind and another, like a bad book cover. Dispense with physical presence and you reach a pure song—the composition and not the boxed instrument.

The Other
"To believe your own thought, to believe that what is true for you in your private heart is true for all men—that is genius."
– Ralph Waldo Emerson: *Self-reliance*

One
Greek and Roman Gods, Celtic Mythology, the epic works of literature, make difficult terrain and One does not feel a natural affinity. Why are they so important? How more important than grass, colours, sounds, sex, animals—things One can taste and test? Why build fantasies when facts are so hard to establish?

I
Metaphor is embedded in the brain. Our body is a kind of metaphor, expressing elements and natural principles. The rational faculty is an instrument of observation and communication, but in order to use it we must learn its capabilities by studying the reported experience of others— their metaphors. To connect with socialised creativity is to expand one's own. So, submit, allow me to open the book.

188. firmaments

The Other
"In my utter impotence to test the authenticity of the report of my senses, to know whether the impressions they make on me correspond with outlying objects, what difference does it make, whether Orion is up there in heaven, or some God paints the image in the firmament of the soul?"
– Ralph Waldo Emerson: *Idealism*

One
What One has seen last week appears entirely different now. A testimony falters before the sceptical eyes of an other. One is never sure of what One knows.

I
What we apperceive depends on the structure, capacity and state of the brain. While humans generally agree on the nature of reality, a variety of individuals demur. How we experience our environment at a given time is determined by circumstance and the line of our attention. There's no final measure of reality. It's an act of faith, drama or delusion to assert a truth.

189. uncommon sense

The Other
"'Mein Vater, mein Vater, und siehst du nicht dort
Erlkönigs Töchter am düstern Ort?' —
'Mein Sohn, mein Sohn, ich seh es genau:
Es scheinen die alten Weiden so grau.'"

"'My father, my father, can't you see over there
Erlking's daughters in the yonder drear?' —
'My son, my son, I surely see
the pallor of age on the willow trees.'"
– Johann Wolfgang von Goethe: *Erlkönig / Erlking*

One
A ghoul walks up the stairs and peers in. Mother's ghost
appears in the corner of the room. Is this madness? One still
follows the daily routine, the mouth answers when spoken
to, the senses share common realities. Sane, it seems.

I
Several conditions give rise to hallucinations, chronic
introspection included. But visions are often considered
gifts. Let's not over-interpret; let's call them company *in
extremis*.

221

190. reason

The Other

"These findings all suggest that the interpretive mechanism of the left hemisphere is always hard at work, seeking the meaning of events. It is constantly looking for order and reason, even when there is none—which leads it continually to make mistakes. It tends to overgeneralize, frequently constructing a potential past as opposed to a true one."
– Michael S. Gazzaniga: *The Split Brain Revisited*

One

One is the crook of a question mark. The landscape is a question mark. Sky is a question mark. Others are a question mark. A question mark ends in a dot, as though every convolution reached an end.

I

Answers pour in and confuse. I swing between blind belief and no belief. There are things I'll never understand with my emotions, but which must be given credence on the basis of strong evidence or reliable reporting. The major questions must be addressed by the inner dialogue, but the facts are more often out there than in here.

191. strategy

The Other
"Viewing reality does not mean making sense of a setup. It means surrendering oneself and triggering an unfathomable transformation."
– Peter Høeg: *Reflection of a Young Man in Balance*

One
These enormous emotions, these blizzards and hurricanes, dwindle periodically to a blank landscape devoid of horizon. Not only this, but no other seems worried, or even aware of their occurrence. Were they real at all then? How does One know when to rest and when to fight?

I
Emotions are encrypted chemical language and we often misjudge their nature and cause. Cease the fevered urgency. Adopt a neutral, reasoning stance. Test everything. In many situations neither battle nor surrender apply.

192. unhinged

The Other
"It is a ridiculous demand which England and America make, that you shall speak so that they can understand you. Neither men nor toadstools grow so."
– Henry David Thoreau: *Walden*

One
One is unhinged. Takes the wrong turning when the route is familiar, says the wrong word when the right one has been iterated to the nth. Sometimes One forgets the name of a daily acquaintance. Is this intellectual deficiency? Or the voiceless world intimating that it is more correct?

I
In the absence of a social imperative, or an other who reminds you of mundane conventions, it's easy to be eccentric and forget details that aren't pertinent to your current obsession. There's a huge fear of 'losing it', but losing what? You remember details others miss. What's lost may be an unwanted prize.

193. warrior

The Other
"Like a prey species animal, many people with autism experience fear as the primary emotion."
– Temple Grandin: *Thinking in Pictures*

One
Every step is dangerous. If the others turn hostile, there is no army to protect. Fall and the ground will open its maw to devour.

I
Something could slice your equilibrium at any time, but you mustn't overestimate the dangers, or underestimate your natural resources. Being inward, you may be well-equipped to learn the strength and flexibility of the mental martial arts.

194. stare and rock

The Other
"I hear and behold God in every object, yet I
    understand God not in the least,
Nor do I understand who there can be more
    wonderful than myself."
– Walt Whitman: *Leaves of Grass*

One
For periods of time One functions according to the basic
rules of survival, buries Oneself in the familiar. One does not
want to know the minds of others or trouble Oneself with
the pandemonium of civilisation. In suspension there is
some peace.

I
I hug myself, being otherwise unhugged, surround myself
with safeties, simply stare and rock. Why not? But alone and
rocking is not the same as accompanied and rocking. With
nobody to prod me, I might, like in-looking eyes, stay that
way.

195. brute sweetness

The Other
"Full many a gem of purest ray serene
The dark unfathom'd caves of ocean bear:
Full many a flower is born to blush unseen,
And waste its sweetness on the desert air."
– Thomas Gray: *Elegy Written in a Country Churchyard*

One
One is a beleaguered animal, craving solace, believing itself smaller than it is, nudging and whining, clumsy and uncouth.

I
Hobbes thought humans brutish and needing to be tamed by society. Rousseau thought them naturally virtuous and noble, and that society corrupts. Neither of these ideas changes the feeling of alienation and the need to touch some other. Here, let me cradle your paw and stroke your lowered head.

196. nomad

The Other
"Nay, be a Columbus to whole new continents and worlds within you, opening new channels, not of trade, but of thought. Every man is the lord of a realm beside which the earthly empire of the Czar is but a petty state, a hammock left by the ice."
– Henry David Thoreau: *Walden*

One
One cannot settle; wanders in search of a foundation that is softer than concrete and safer than bog.

I
In the final analysis, is there anything but the home within, of which all outward structure is a reflection? Can I found a portable household with the means to a living, faithful affection and some restful times? It might sustain as well as any shared homestead.

197. fogswim

The Other
"What difference would it make, Bonds asked the *USA Today* reporter, 'if I changed and started acting nicer to people? ... I just wish people would accept me for who I am. Why should I change? ... I don't care what people say or what the media portrays me to be, I'm proud of who I am. The Bible says you don't have to be nice, or not nice. Just speak the truth. Jesus always spoke the truth. Not everybody liked him either.'"
– Barry Bonds of the San Francisco Giants: *USA Today*

One
The supply of friends has dwindled to a few distant contacts. When they left, it did not seem they were needed, but then absence poured in under the closed door, like a sea of dense, cloying fog.

I
It seems that absence is your home. But such a nebulous medium can either consume or disperse. If you must live here, you could learn to fogswim, moving with each subtle twist.

198. perfume of the void

The Other
"At the core of the Perennial Philosophy we find four fundamental doctrines. First: the phenomenal world of matter and of individualized consciousness—the world of things and animals and men and even gods—is the manifestation of a Divine Ground within which all partial realities have their being, and apart from which they would be non-existent."
– Aldous Huxley: *Introduction to Bhagavad-Gita*

One
Could walk by a building every day and not be aware of it. Could live in a location for years and never see the neighbour's garden. It's not that One's hermetic world is so diverse; often it is a blank field. However, there is a capacity to feel atmospheres. An incorporeal blow to the head on entering an ashram in Colorado, a whole-body response to the voice of Alison Kraus.

I
For the Buddhist, the perfume of the Void penetrates each day as a subtle air. It dwells in all forms and is the form. We know that the air has chemical components that shift as we move. We could think of ourselves as streams in a sea where each movement affects all others and our encounters are dialogues between constituents of the tide.

199. the will of the wild

The Other
"We live our lives inscrutably included within the streaming mutual life of the universe."
– Martin Buber: *I and Thou*

One
One experiences nature as an unstopped vowel. It stirs no curiosity, infuses no drive. Without end or beginning, enormous, it is ungraspable. One could be lost in it, sucked into a thoughtless, terrifying no-time.

I
Faced with mute nature, you become silent. It's not your will that predominates, but the will of the wild. In neuroscience, they might say that the brain slips into default mode and apperception is minimised.

200. off-grid

The Other
"When logics die,
The secret of the soil grows through the eye...."
– Dylan Thomas: *Light Breaks Where No Sun Shines*

One
They enquire about One's position on politics and religion,
where One stands on moral issues. The truth is that the feet
stand on this patch of ground and the thoughts labour
landless in the virgin air. There is no position that cannot be
shifted and no issue that makes a pivot of the psyche.

I
This is not selfishness as commonly understood, but rather
a tendency to filter everything through the senses.
Experience is the primary source of information. Words like
politics, religion, morality, have become high street
reifications and carry little precise meaning. Show me the
issue and I can give a reaction, but not necessarily an
ideological position. The affairs of the planet are too large
for précis, and I'm too small to be placed on the map.

201. unjust deserts

The Other
"Nothing living is a means: all is automatic, spontaneous, justified by whatever it tends to and loves."
– George Santayana: *My Host the World*

One
That weight in the chest is guilt. Never sure what is deserved. Having chosen severance from others, it feels as if One's only rights are those that are stolen. Like the social outcast who must carry out night-time raids for food.

I
How can one possibly measure what's deserved? People can't and don't perform equally. It's commonly asserted that inexhaustible workers deserve the fruits of their labour, and altruists that of their virtue, but this is a constructed notion of payback. Mightn't the solitary, responsible for herself, protecting herself from harm, 'deserve' the fruit of her omissions?

202. if loner I am

The Other
"I really do believe I am lost to all social intercourse. I am quite incapable of conducting a prolonged vigorously developed conversation with any individual, except in certain exceptional, appallingly exceptional cases."
– Franz Kafka: *Franz Kafka, Letters to Felice*

One
One is inept and unwitty in conversation; never gains the desired connection. The only route to spontaneity is to clothe Oneself in drugs or delusions. Then all the entities come, those avatars released from the blasted chambers of the brain.

I
Would it be worthwhile to establish a mode of behaviour that would cater to the needs of others? Would my own direction, such as it is, be lost? Is that my inherent dilemma: whether to be concerned with others or with myself? It seems that neither brings peace. Should I involve myself with those of the same mindset and find satisfaction that way? It might be possible to express myself honestly in well-chosen company. But a company of loners is a paradox. If loner I am.

PART 3: PERSPECTIVE

I ...

is always in danger of toppling.
We bolster it upholster it
strap it round with a gun belt
and pin it with ropes.
This babel tower leans according to the
wind
tries to imagine itself in another place
with a different style of window
but it can't leave.
Its one leg can only stand or fall.

toppling

203. picture

A girl in a green terrain. No perspective. The grass and hedges might as well be a carpet shaken by the sky, and she something small enough to imagine it is making tracks. There is no sense of another presence, and as yet no intimation of danger.

204. retreat

Danger. Large people are noisy. The girl retreats into the night-time sense and daytime reality of grass. No words explain.

205. play

The girl is strong, has energy and wants to play. Because she has no companions, she takes her bearings from the ground and builds herself a simple world.

206. graceless

She wants someone to arrive on her carpet and laugh, but those in her environs are colourless, speak tonelessly, and have nothing like the grace of meadows.

207. exhibits

Her life is a museum of puzzled moments: this face with the casual look of disapproval; that careless sentence. The rooms themselves are forgettable.

208. grove

Trees bow to her like royal attendants. The ground is cushioned with flowers that are blue and purple, yellow in the centre. Bushes grow untended, butterflies arrive with the summer heat.

209. society

Others stop and look. The ambience is disturbed. They ask why she sits alone, squandering her thoughts on the improbable, why the precious demeanour and measured manners. Why doesn't she know how to use and be used? Why doesn't she want to fit?

210. conversation
They finger the leaves of the trees and don't feel them. Then they finger and feel so intensely that they're lost to her. They talk about their hearts. They ask about hers.

211. association
They want to start a club. They'll let her in. But she understands that she must decimate her grove. There's that purple bush she lays her head under day after day—she mustn't do that, it's odd.

212. regular
They'll reduce her to a cipher with a regulated tone, singing in a choir, sweet among many. She'll lose her singular seat among beings that question nothing.

213. jumble
All information confuses her. The saying of things is always right and then always wrong. Doing is only doing.

214. sniff and spit
She's only, on the face of it, a shy country girl, as yet unaccepted into society, unschooled in the power methods of the race. She sniffs, sticks her little finger in her ear, spits on the footpath. She doesn't say, 'Pardon me'.

215. uncivilised
She's easiest among the less civilised—transients and the rough-skinned in chippers and pubs. With them there's no issue of acceptance, no constant weighing of worth.

216. annexed
Others are always intrusive, as though she owed them more than herself. She succumbs to their assertions, forgets she's an autonomous instrument with a capacity for occupying space.

217. conundrum
Where is the centre of the principle of growth, the fixed pivot of existence? She's held to this question like a frozen chrysalis.

218. come
Above all, she wants to be truthful. Next, she wants to be intimate. She stares at her basket of fruit. She can't bring it to the marketplace.

219. vacant
Being alone isn't the same as being in herself. She evicts herself from her moments, the better to survive them. She stands in her own light.

220. you
No matter how close they come, she finds herself at a great distance. The back of her head pulls her into a long lean. Is that why she can't look at a face and say, 'you'?

221. janus
She tries, but the affairs of the world don't hold her interest. She loses the thread of sounds, listening to the silence before her birth.

another place

222. ceasefire
I wake to silence. A stretching, seamless peace. Stunned by fluid ease and the absence of argument, this is a free land.

223. unstopped
for a brief but wide moment i know no punctuation no punching home of the fact of my great lone voyage stillness is a shocking thing that you can claim it

224. treasure
Is this what was meant by the crock of gold, a treasure to be won if you could only keep hold of the messenger? I lose attention and can't regain the spot. Now the bubbling-up of voices, like a hot pain under the skin of the earth.

225. inspired
But that moment of peace has wormed the memory, like the seducing taste of a holiday dish. Could I allow a state of no dialogue? Imagine floating in silent space, deep in ruminating blue and its long, balming out-breath.

226. chott
The place before me is a dry salt lake, flat and charged, like the pause between tortures. Its white landscape, long abandoned by the sea, serves no purpose except to lack.

227. lethe
Not that the chott knows what it lacks. It doesn't recall. There's only the insistent pulse of aimless desire, the fluid history forgotten. Every turn of the weather is a surprise, lived without the savvy of experience. Watch these words die young in the crevices of its face.

228. land
The chott challenges every inch of resolve. I force myself to step onto it. I sit far out, where there's nothing in any

direction but deadening white. This is a location too, although nothing marks it.

229. barren
The bare land is more desolate than silent space. I expect ground to lead somewhere, to speak the language of production. When nothing sprouts, the body clutches itself pitifully, like a small, unloved child.

230. frontier
Is this the territory of *One*? It has the timbre of that voice but lacks its rage. If there were a dragon to fight, I'd be more at ease. My task would be clear.

231. endless
I could invent a quest, but it would remain an invention. Success would be illusory. The end, if there were an end, would be a blank wall, the parched lake standing on its hind legs.

232. how
One's first question remains the issue. How am I to live? I lie prostrate and let silence turn my flesh colourless. I must not be afraid. Fear is what conquers.

233. neutral
One rises and recedes underground. Nothing happens from above. The intoned blue has a mind only to itself. Between salt and sky is a neutral matrix.

234. plus
Ground minus. Before what is. I start to walk. Still no landmark. But these visions: a slim woman with short hair, crouched pensively on a river-bank; a small girl walking away through tall grass. They're at my hand, at a hundred metres, in every direction.

235. tiny

So what if I'm a lone traveller? It appears that the immense, metabolic world doesn't care whether I lie, sit or walk. I'm a microscopic theme. But tiny is mother to large.

236. full circle

I've barely listened to *The Other*. Who questions my right to exist? Turn 360 degrees. Turn again. There's nobody here who rejects me. No obstacle. Only mirages cast by the fickle eye of *One*.

237. soldier

I'm waiting for a compass and a map, to be dropped from the sky by envoys from a loving homeland. Maybe it's all a game in the hands of a giant, and I'm to be the hero.

238. hypostasis

The grumblings of *One* cause physical pain, as though they could hypostasise. There's hardly room in the body for both of us. I'll be lost.

239. run

I start to run. Nowhere. There's nowhere to run. Run without reason. Run because there is breath, because there are legs.

240. task

I live in the limbs, and in the stomach where *One* sucks and twists. The lungs must breathe round the shard *One* has lodged in the chest. This is something to achieve.

241. a different sky

The Other has spoken of task and called it heroism. So a different sky must exist, smiling on similars. *The Other* has spread maps under my feet, but I've skimmed them like hurdles, touching down in rare spots.

242. unchartered
If there's no one map, there's no one way, perhaps no best way. What will decide my direction? If I only reach small, inglorious stations, who's to say the journey was wasted?

243. loosening
The lack of presence begins to feel like freedom. I speak to I, keep talking, while *One* mutters in the bones, stinking of sabotage. I tell myself there are only the tragedies I allow.

244. descend
The ground begins to slope. It makes a tunnel to receive me. There are patterns on the walls and each one deserves examination. I slow.

245. neophyte
Becoming the acts of observation and movement. Each time a foot is raised, it falls at a slightly different pace, feels a different level of force. When the eye changes focus, it finds something new.

246. conversant
I converse with my environment. There's nothing to say to *One,* except that I am.

247. outlook
I am the centre and I look out from here. I am also an *Other.* I allow myself to be seen. I am not the creator of the world or of myself. I need not be ashamed. I dwell. I ask.

248. inglow
This tunnel hardly leads to a hidden cave. It seems to have swallowed a sun.

249. blur
Is it underground at all? Has the soil become something else? Water? Has it dissolved in itself? The outline of my body blurs. This is what they speak of. Involvement.

250. flow
Feet merge with their tread. Hands become lost in what they touch. Body belongs to its matrix. I seep into old sand.

251. face to face
It's my face, this ground. I am the water bowl. I inhale what rains and it becomes me. I contain *One* and I am *One*.

252. pre-frontal
I observe, direct the emotions, record patterns. I'm pragmatic. I shock-absorb.

253. emissary
One is the anchor and the spawning ground. I'm sent out on a long leash. Running towards the horizon, I'm a child on a planet full of toys.

254. explore
The truth is outside. It's there that the impulse began. In here is only the interplay of all that has fallen. I face *The Other*. *The Other* looks through my eye.

255. adventure
A knife tip presses through the sky and keeps cutting. Its gleaming blade holds my attention. I cast a line through the gap and climb through. As I thought, there are other worlds.

stand

256. thoroughfare

There are constant airy voices, a million different streams, and I a drifting island, subject to landings and colonies.

257. firsts

They talk of what's acceptable and forbidden. By whose say? I grew in deserted fields where no voice chased me with data and principle. My conventions were formed by the attitudes of light and the soil that tickled my hands. What comes first stays first. But I listen.

258. director

I am a study, a documentary. I live and observe myself doing it; I speak of myself; I replay myself; I plan future speeches and actions; I speculate.

259. no problem

I work hard to acquire normal habits, keep my little finger from screwing into my ear, swallow my spit. I understand that others are not so different. I'm acceptable now, and the corners of my house are bright. But this gentle land is something of a desert too. I must find a problem to solve.

260. commerce

One paces the backroom, sings, knocks, whispers, shouts— my internal weather. Out among the public, I'm calm enough to look both ways. I'm a saleable commodity, adaptable as a stem cell. *One* can't compromise, must sound the self or die.

261. true love

A philanderer, I leave *One* alone while I have affairs. I come home to our persistent love and those unsettling moods. I'll never leave, *One* knows that, but our frequent tussles have made us both afraid.

262. suffer
Is there any mind that rests easy all the time? The quest for Nirvana began as an awareness of suffering, but why shouldn't we suffer?

263. satisfied
A so-called resolved life has difficulties too. From where comes the notion that our lives are not satisfactory? They must be satisfactory—we have nothing else.

264. compelled
There are many stories of how people destroy relationships because of some compulsion or destructive belief. I swore it wouldn't happen to me. But here I am, alone for no good reason, knowing others who are also alone, unable to reach out and make us better.

265. questions
Christian mystics are wedded to Christ or his mother. Buddhist monks are one with the universal consciousness. Their shared aim is to be united with a larger entity. What distinguishes our lifestyles is that they have a belief and a set practice, whereas I have only questions. If their beliefs are fact, I'm as accompanied as they. If not, we're all alone.

266. endure
Every so often I look up from my lone table and feel the weight of emptiness. I have great desire but only a nebulous goal. I mustn't seek company for its own sake before I know my direction.

267. war dance
I turn up the music and dive into a dance. I lose myself in sound. It smokes out my embedded enemies.

268. quotidian
What's so attractive about commerce that people must constantly boast of their ability to find bargains, organise finance, buy large pieces of furniture and high-technology products? My quest is not of its day.

269. flagellant
In the early morning I'm flayed by what I want to forget—that I've missed opportunities by being too inward; that I'm mediocre; that my beliefs have been onanistic delusions; that I've been wrong in crucial judgements and self-destructive in dismissals; that I generate my own problems. I whimper, unbelieving, that these are only perceptions, and haul my attention to something else. What can't be changed can be wrapped in new action.

270. student
I study the subjects that puzzle me. Knowledge liberates. I provide myself with constant stimulation so that the claw of the voracious *One* doesn't close again. This is as much in the pursuit of truth as of happiness.

271. lamped
Who am I fooling? The prospect of yet another evening alone turns me cold and trembling. The great eye of sociability sweeps the world for defectors. I can only crouch, lamped rabbit that I am, and try to recall the rudiments of motion.

272. oneiric haven
Dense, dangerous, or bright, all dreams are a boon. I hold to what the night has allowed. Rooted in genes and spontaneous associations, my subconscious is home.

273. even
Alone in the house and no longer anxious at the silence. No chattering in the body's environs. Without words, silent or sounded, I'm an even breath, a perceiving entity. That's all.

274. syndrome
My needs and desires are fundamentally those of everyone else. The difference is that I'm programmed to resist the imposition of a common language. This is painful, but no worse than an allergy.

275. collateral
There are always streams of life that continue undammed and unconcerned. My inner environment may be fraught with the nature of earthquakes while others swim calm-faced, moving with an easy current. In the long-term this is reassuring.

276. style-less
I've seen wisdom as something gained by being unfashionable, unpopular and physically restrained—characteristics of the loner. Does it matter? I'll forget the dictates of style and allow my nature to reach for what it wants.

277. dice
To choose one option destroys the others and creates a station. But without a station there's no context and no perceptible entity; I'm not even on the grid of my own mind. If I choose carefully, I'll gain something that I value. If not, whatever I miss or lose will be taken up by somebody else. Time will anyhow absorb.

278. non-starter
Some people are so in love with a goal that they isolate themselves in its pursuit. But the lack of a goal creates a deeper isolation, akin to bereavement. I've never begun to be involved, but I set goals because it's a way to live.

279. tower
The light in the watchtower is always on. I am my own bodyguard, general and envoy. I'm loyal. My secrets are safe with me.

280. tiptoe

The general expectation is that I understand and employ the subtle manoeuvres necessary to the social process. If I don't, I'm either in the wrong social stream or on the wrong side of the madhouse wall. I carefully tread a path between.

281. melt

A man and child in a café, each with a fluid, speaking body. They're slow and tentative in their talk. The man's expression is so tender I feel heat in that frozen place on the inner globe. Ice, dangerously, turns to water.

282. slate

That I'm loved is something I must accept without feeling its truth. It displays itself in actions I can see. I remind myself every day, because every day wipes the one before.

283. abide

I have abiding tendencies and imperatives. I dislike green olives, I love mushrooms, I hate certain tones of voice. I'm unhappy with certain people, calm and relaxed with others. I have memories. I might train myself to new perceptions and behaviours, but I'll remain a distinct entity with old motivations.

284. belong

Loner or not, I have context and history. I have a country, and a body that expresses genetic identity. I didn't occur without source, however I might wish to assert it.

285. care

Nobody else will ensure the quality of my life. If I don't care for it, it will end up drunk and begging on a bustling bridge.

286. back off
I have clung to what unsettled me, as if that was a settling practice. As though keeping the enemies close made them manageable. But when it comes to internal dangers, distance is more effective.

287. dual
I must be two: agent and observer. The lone life can then be sustained, plotted to the last step for fear of injury; or dotted with challenge and sudden changes. As we wish.

288. teacher
The majority accept the prevailing social structures as though they were natural phenomena, fundamentally correct. An outsider, I question all assumptions. I can be a teacher, then, reveal them to themselves.

289. roses
They tell me to take up gardening, but activity isn't the only requirement. I need an other, in my house or head, to convince me of my relevance.

290. identify
Yesterday morning my name was *Fit*. In the afternoon I was *Mentor* for a while, then *Organiser*, then *Inept*. In the night I was *Sleeping Wolf*, with a wolf's dreams of mountains. Today, when I woke, *Suicide* was my epithet and then *Soldier*. Later, who knows?

291. snatched
Why should the world not own me? I'm far from my first home, taken by the bandits of confusion, dressed in desire, when once I only had body.

292. the price
I can only experience liberty if I'm often unaccompanied and without duty. For this I might forego healing caresses and sexual approbation. But there are many kinds of partnership, and gaps in the tightest weaves.

293. bring it on
Whatever caused this idiosyncratic mind, whether genes, environment, or chemical machinations, I'm likely to possess it for as long as I live. Victory begins with accepting the unavoidable.

294. re-cycle
There's a sound outside the window. I look out and see a man putting a bag in his rubbish bin. What if his life were involved with mine? What if his consciousness weren't superfluous to me?

295. ride out
In unfamiliar territory, I search and make a vehicle from any available materials. Like a pioneer, I prospect for a new home.

296. eden
What looks like a cave to you is a portal to Paradise. Not where I'm an angel, but where I'm a glutted, guileful animal; and then again a sweet, light-as-air, flowing-as-water lover. I'll cease the denial of my familiars—insidious rats of doubt, snake-like survival responses. Cats arrive stare-eyed, intent on themselves and all that will bolster them, never afraid to follow their logic, unashamed of the blood dripping from their mouths as they gracefully lick their paws.

297. dragon
This unshareable store of gems is a thing to be proud of, brilliant in its self-generated light.

298. art
The daily routines, uninspiring as they may seem, are at least in my possession. Could I elevate them to the level of beauty, transmute them to the expression of their finer principles? This would be a form of art.

299. set in stone
Ephemeral feelings are made too solid in conversation. Afterwards I'm left with monoliths for mental scenery. I'd better speak to the selfish, the amnesiac, or the objective.

300. gyre
I can accept the periodic recurrence of a blank view. In between, there's activity and the possibility of achievement, as if what's popularly called 'a life' is happening. This turning may be all the life there is.

301. real estate
I search my interior for another inhabitant and find none. I'm a house between tenancies. The naked floor is whatever I make of it—bed or flying carpet, skating rink or mirror. I'm not settled, but safe, it seems.

302. animist
Whatever I've done and learned, communicated or not, remains in the world as experience. How can I say that humans are more important than the air that has bathed, the river that has buoyed, or the grass that has fallen to their blades?

303. abandon

I light a candle in an empty room and let it dance by itself like a shoreless sea. I need not know what happens next: whether yellow seeps into transparency, or pink, or red; whether the air pulls up a seat, huddling closer to itself, winter-aware. If there's barbecue or furnace need not concern me. That room, that empty room, that empty room with the candle in it, that empty room with the candle and the air in it and the colours and the winter warmth can look to itself.

APPENDICES

SOURCES FOR THE QUOTATIONS
(Refer to the Bibliography for book editions)

Epigraphs:
W. H. Auden: 'The Riddle', *Collected Poems*, p. 258/9.
Michel de Montaigne: *Les Essais* / *The Essays*, Ch. 39: 'De la Solitude' / 'Of Solitude'. Translation by Aonghus McGovern.

PART 1: IF ONE IS TO LIVE

1. Albert Camus: *The Plague*, p. 63.
2. Henry David Thoreau: *Walden* (Conclusion), *Walden and Civil Disobedience*, p. 382.
3. John Cage: *Silence: Lectures and Writings by John Cage*, Wesleyan University Press, 1961, p. 8. Quoted in Sara Maitland, *A Book of Silence*, 2008, p. 26.
4. Søren Kierkegaard: 'The Sickness unto Death', *The Essential Kierkegaard*, p. 351.
5. Marcus Aurelius: *Meditations* (1997), XI, p. 54.
6. Anneli Rufus: *Party of One*, p. 243.
7. Thomas Moore: *The Care of the Soul*, p. 186.
8. Jean-Jacques Rousseau: *Confessions*, p. 457.
9. Philip Larkin: 'Strangers', *Collected Poems* (1990), p. 40.
10. Ciaran Carson: 'Two to Tango', *Collected Poems*, p. 224.
11. Andrée Chedid: 'Landscapes' / 'Paysages', *Selected Poems of Andrée Chedid*, p. 10–15, translated by Judy Pfau Cochran.
12. Heinrich Cornelius Agrippa von Nettesheim (1486–1535): quoted in Jorge Luis Borges, 'The Nothingness of Personality', *The Total Library: Non-Fiction 1922–1986*, p. 5.
13. Walt Whitman: 'A Noiseless Patient Spider'. Online at: http://classiclit.about.com/
14. Michael Hartnett: 'The Naked Surgeon', *A Necklace of Wrens*, p. 115.
15. Albert Camus: *The Myth of Sisyphus*, p. 29.

16. Bernard Levin: *Enthusiasms*, p. 15.
17. Bernard J. Baars and Nicole M. Gage: *Cognition, Brain and Consciousness*, p. 294.
18. John Cacioppo and William Patrick: *Loneliness,* p. 216.
19. Jean-Jacques Rousseau: *Émile*, p. 174.
20. Jean-Jacques Rousseau: *The Reveries of the Solitary Walker*, p. 5/6.
21. Philip Larkin: 'Vers de Société', *Collected Poems* (2003), p. 147.
22. Augustine of Hippo, c. BCE 400: quoted in David Ewing Duncan, *The Calendar*, p. 73.
23. Rainer Maria Rilke: uncited letter, quoted in Gaston Bachelard, *The Poetics of Space*, p. 203.
24. Tenzin Palmo: quoted in Vicki Mackenzie, *Cave in the Snow*, p. 166.
25. C. G. Jung: *The Undiscovered Self*, p. 21.
26. Diane Purkiss: *Troublesome Things*, p. 99 (spoken by a girl with multiple personalities).
27. Alexander Pope: 'Solitude: An Ode'. Online at: http://www.poetryfoundation.org/poem/175899
28. William Cowper: 'The Solitude of Alexander Selkirk', Francis T. Palgrave, ed., *The Golden Treasury*, 1875. Online at: http://www.bartleby.com/106/160.html
29. Ciaran Carson: 'St Ciaran's Island', *Collected Poems*, p. 24.
30. Marcus Aurelius: *Meditations* (1997), p. 87.
31. Eric Hoffer: *The True Believer: Thoughts on the Nature of Mass Movements*, Part 3, p. 59.
32. Anthony Storr: *The Integrity of the Personality*, p. 37.
33. Marcus Aurelius: *Meditations* (2004), p. 11.
34. Vladimir Nabokov: *The Luzhin Defense*, p. 228.
35. Jean-Jacques Rousseau: *The Social Contract, The Social Contract and the Discourses*, p. 219.
36. Emily Dickinson: '126', *The Complete Poems of Emily Dickinson*, p. 59.
37. Philip Larkin: *New York Review of Books, Volume 53*, 2006. Quoted in Josephine Hart, *Catching Life by the Throat*, p. 124.

38. Peter Abbs: *The Development of Autobiography in Western Culture: from Augustine to Rousseau,* unpublished thesis, University of Sussex, 1986, p. 130. Quoted in Anthony Storr: *Solitude,* p. 80.
39. Temple Grandin: *Emergence: Labeled Autistic,* p. 106.
40. *Tibetan Book of the Dead,* translated by Gyurme Dorje, p. 78.
41. Ralph Waldo Emerson: 'Self-reliance', *Selected Essays,* p. 199.
42. Emily Dickinson: '35', *The Complete Poems of Emily Dickinson,* p. 22.
43. Daniel Dennett: *Consciousness Explained,* p. 174.
44. Michael Hartnett: 'Tao, 16', *Translations,* p. 14.
45. Dylan Thomas: 'Light Breaks Where No Sun Shines', *Collected Poems 1934–1952,* p. 21.
46. Anneli Rufus: *Party of One: The Loner's Manifesto,* p. 100.
47. Henry David Thoreau: *Walden* (Conclusion), *Walden and Civil Disobedience,* p. 376.
48. Michael Hartnett: 'Tao, 50', *Translations,* p. 21.
49. Temple Grandin: *Thinking in Pictures,* p. 183.
50. Jorge Luis Borges: 'Everything and Nothing', *Labyrinths,* p. 284.
51. Walt Whitman: *Leaves of Grass,* lls 526–529, p. 42.
52. Ralph Waldo Emerson: 'The Over-soul', *Selected Essays,* p. 213.
53. Søren Kierkegaard: 'Either/Or, A Fragment of Life', *The Essential Kierkegaard,* p. 57.
54. Michael Hartnett: 'The Naked Surgeon', lls 5–8, *A Necklace of Wrens,* p. 103.
55. Ralph Waldo Emerson: 'Self-reliance', *Selected Essays,* p. 176.
56. Sara Maitland: *A Book of Silence,* p. 3.
57. Michael Newton: *Savage Girls and Wild Boys,* p. 90.
58. Adrienne Rich: 'Cartographies of Silence', *The Dream of a Common Language,* p. 16.
59. Daniel Dennett: *Consciousness Explained,* p. 179.

60. Amy Turner: *Sunday Times*, 29 June 2008—feature on Burt Pugach and Linda Riss. Online at: http://orange pulpfilms.livejournal.com/23611.html (The film, *Crazy Love*, 2007, tells the story of Burt's violent possessiveness.)
61. Eric Hoffer: *The True Believer: Thoughts on the Nature of Mass Movements*, No. 77, p. 99.
62. Jean-Jacques Rousseau: *The Reveries of the Solitary Walker*, p. 132.
63. Friedrich Nietzsche: *Thus Spake Zarathustra*, p. 144.
64. J. M. Coetzee: *In the Heart of the Country*, p. 13.
65. Oscar Wilde: *The Picture of Dorian Gray* (2008), p. 20.
66. Jean-Jacques Rousseau: 'Last Reply' (to M. Charles Bordes), in *The Discourses and Other Early Political Writings*, translated and edited by Victor Gourevitch, p. 66.
67. Anthony Storr: *Solitude*, p. 15.
68. Thomas Merton: *Seven Storey Mountain*, p. 330.
69. Jean-Jacques Rousseau: *The Reveries of the Solitary Walker*, p. 95.
70. Henry David Thoreau: *Walden* ('Economy'), *Walden and Civil Disobedience*, p. 122.
71. Henry David Thoreau: *Walden* ('Solitude'), *Walden and Civil Disobedience*, p. 178.
72. Dylan Thomas: 'Ears in the Turrets Hear', *Collected Poems 1934–1952*, p. 53.
73. Henry David Thoreau: quoted in Introduction, *Walden and Civil Disobedience*, p. 29.
74. Ralph Waldo Emerson: 'Self-reliance', *Selected Essays*, p. 181.
75. Oscar Wilde: *The Picture of Dorian Gray* (2003), p. 21.
76. Louis MacNeice: 'Autumn Journal', XVII, lls 37–40, *Collected Poems*, p. 142.
77. Virginia Woolf: *A Room of One's Own,* p. 92, speaking of Duchess Margaret of Newcastle, who, she thought, never reached her artistic potential.
78. Louis MacNeice: 'Eclogue from Iceland', *Collected Poems*, p. 77.

79. Primo Levi: *The Periodic Table*, p. 5.
80. Eric Hoffer: *Reflections on the Human Condition*, No. 140, p. 76.
81. George MacDonald: *Lilith* (1895), online at: http://www.gutenberg.org/files/1640/1640-h/1640-h.htm
82. Arthur Schopenhauer: *The World as Will and Idea*, p. 180.
83. Henry David Thoreau: *Walden* (Conclusion), *Walden and Civil Disobedience*, p. 377.
84. Jean-Jacques Rousseau: *Émile*, p. 198.
85. Jean-Jacques Rousseau: *The Reveries of the Solitary Walker*, p. 70.
86. Philip Larkin: 'Vers de Société', *Collected Poems* (2003), p. 147.
87. *Tibetan Book of the Dead*, translated by Gyurme Dorje, p. 14.
88. Henry David Thoreau: *Walden* ('Solitude'), *Walden and Civil Disobedience*, p. 180.
89. Michel de Montaigne: *Les Essais / The Essays*, Ch. 39: 'De la Solitude' / 'Of Solitude', translation by Aonghus McGovern.
90. Danah Zohar: *The Quantum Self*, p. 209.
91. Danah Zohar: *The Quantum Self*, p. 159.
92. Thomas Merton: *The Seven Storey Mountain*, p. 330.
93. Temple Grandin: *Emergence: Labeled Autistic*, p. 29.
94. Michel de Montaigne: *Les Essais / The Essays*, Ch. 39: 'De la Solitude' / 'Of Solitude', translation by Aonghus McGovern.
95. Michel Houellebecq: spoken by Daniel 1 in *The Possibility of an Island*, p. 190.
96. Søren Kierkegaard: 'Either/Or, A Fragment of Life', *The Essential Kierkegaard,* p. 39.
97. Johann Wolfgang von Goethe: 'Erlkönig' / 'Erlking', English version by Máighréad Medbh. Text online at: http://german.about.com/library/blerlking.htm
98. Franz Kafka: Letter to Felice, July 7, 1913, *Franz Kafka, Letters to Felice* (1973), p. 279. Quoted in *I am a Memory Come Alive,* p. 88.

99. William Byrd: *Alone*, quoted in Sara Maitland, *A Book of Silence*, p. 83.
100. Michael Hartnett: 'Short Mass', *Collected Poems, Volume 1*, p. 19.
101. Walt Whitman: *Leaves of Grass*, lls 1120–1122.

PART 2: THE DANGEROUS WORLD

102. William Blake: 'Infant Sorrow', *Selected Poems*, p. 37.
103. Eric Hoffer: *The True Believer: Thoughts on the Nature of Mass Movements*, No. 2, p. 6.
104. Leo Barsani: Introduction to Sigmund Freud, *Civilization and its Discontents*, p. vii.
105. Thomas Merton: *The Seven Storey Mountain*, p. 133.
106. Henry David Thoreau: *Walden* ('Solitude'), *Walden and Civil Disobedience*, p. 182.
107. Henry David Thoreau: *Walden* ('Sounds'), *Walden and Civil Disobedience*, p. 156.
108. Jean-Jacques Rousseau: *The Reveries of the Solitary Walker*, p. 32.
109. Rainer Maria Rilke: 'The Words of the Lord to John on Patmos' / 'Die Worte Des Herrn An Johannes Auf Patmos'. English version by Máighréad Medbh. German text in *Uncollected Poems*, 1997, p. 118.
110. Emily Dickinson: '777', *The Complete Poems*, p. 379.
111. Eric Hoffer: *The True Believer: Thoughts on the Nature of Mass Movements*, No. 31, p. 35.
112. John Keats: Letter to George and Thomas, December 21, 1817. In H. E. Rollins ed., *Letters of John Keats, Vol. 1*, 1958, p. 193–4. Also online at: http://www.mrbauld.com/negcap.html
113. David Hume: quoted in Oliver Sacks, *The Man who Mistook His Wife for a Hat*, p. 29/30.
114. Friedrich Nietzsche: *The Birth of Tragedy*, p. 60.
115. Rainer Maria Rilke: untitled poem, first line: 'Unwissend, vor dem Himmel meines Lebens....'

English version by Máighréad Medbh. German text in *Uncollected Poems*, 1997, p. 54.

116. Henry David Thoreau: *Walden* ('Solitude'), *Walden and Civil Disobedience*, p. 177.
117. Ralph Waldo Emerson: 'History', *Selected Essays*, p. 149.
118. Ralph Waldo Emerson: 'The Over-soul', *Selected Essays*, p. 222.
119. Marcus Aurelius: *Meditations* (2004), p. 13.
120. Ben Stoltzfus: *Lacan and Literature: Purloined Texts*, p. 20.
121. Michael Newton: *Savage Girls and Wild Boys*, p. 98, describing the 'wild boy of Aveyron'.
122. Ian McEwan: *Saturday*, p. 92.
123. Ralph Waldo Emerson: 'Self-reliance', *Selected Essays*, p. 179.
124. Michel Houellebecq: *Platform*, p. 130.
125. Jean-Paul Sartre: *Being and Nothingness*, p. 291.
126. Philip Larkin: 'Dockery and Son', *Collected Poems* (2003), p. 108.
127. Ralph Waldo Emerson: *Selected Prose and Poetry* (1969), quoted in James Geary, *We Are What We Think*, p. 148.
128. Adrienne Rich: 'Transcendental Etude', *The Dream of a Common Language*, p. 72.
129. Eric Hoffer: *The True Believer: Thoughts on the Nature of Mass Movements*, No. 45, p. 64.
130. Walt Whitman: *Leaves of Grass*, lls 413–415.
131. Jean-Jacques Rousseau: *Émile*, p. 191.
132. Maria Montessori: Montessori Scotts Valley website: http://www.montessorisv.com/maria-montessori.htm
133. Michel Houellebecq: *H.P. Lovecraft Against the World, Against Life*, p. 29.
134. Douglas Hofstadter: *I am a Strange Loop*, p. 250.
135. Milan Kundera: *Immortality*, p. 35.
136. George Santayana: *My Host the World*, p. 153.
137. Danah Zohar: *The Quantum Self*, p. 106.

138. Philip Larkin: 'Best Society', *Collected Poems* (1990), p. 56/7.
139. Anthony Storr: *Solitude*, p. 72.
140. Daniel Dennett: *Consciousness Explained*, p. 423.
141. Philip Larkin: 'Vers de Société', *Collected Poems* (2003), p. 147.
142. Ciaran Carson: 'Two to Tango', *Collected Poems*, p. 222.
143. Henry David Thoreau: 'Civil Disobedience', *Walden and Civil Disobedience,* p. 396.
144. Virginia Woolf: *A Room of One's Own*, p. 98.
145. M. A. Screech: Introduction to Michel de Montaigne, *The Complete Essays*, p. xviii.
146. Jean-Jacques Rousseau: *Émile*, p. 7.
147. David J. Wallin: *Attachment in Psychotherapy*, p. 71.
148. Jean-Jacques Rousseau: *The Reveries of the Solitary Walker*, p. 83.
149. Eric Matthews: *Mind: Key Concepts in Philosophy*, p. 126.
150. Philip Larkin: 'Wants', *Collected Poems* (2003), p. 52.
151. John Milton: *Paradise Lost*, Book 8, Adam, lls 364–366.
152. Jorge Luis Borges: 'The Nothingness of Personality', *The Total Library: Non-Fiction 1922–1986*, p. 3.
153. Jorge Luis Borges: 'Everything and Nothing', *Labyrinths*, p. 284.
154. Elizabeth Bishop: 'In the Waiting Room', *Complete Poems*, p. 159.
155. Douglas Hofstadter: *I am a Strange Loop*, p. 251.
156. W. B. Yeats: 'The Mask', *Collected Poems*, p. 106.
157. Eric Hoffer: *The True Believer: Thoughts on the Nature of Mass Movements*, No. 7, p. 12.
158. J. M. Coetzee: *In the Heart of the Country,* p. 79.
159. Emily Jane Brontë: 'Oh, thy bright eyes must answer now', The Brontë Sisters, *Selected Poems*, p. 79.
160. Franz Kafka: *Letters to Felice* (1974), p. 271. Quoted in Anthony Storr, *Solitude*, p. 101.
161. Jean-Jacques Rousseau: *The Social Contract and the Discourses*, p. 115.

162. Friedrich Nietzsche: *Thus Spake Zarathustra*, p. 89.
163. Sara Maitland: *The Book of Silence*, p. 17.
164. Jean-Jacques Rousseau: *The Reveries of the Solitary Walker*, p. 37.
165. Ralph Waldo Emerson: 'Self-Reliance', *Selected Essays*, p. 178.
166. Meng-hu: *Hermitary* website, © 2010, http://www.hermitary.com/articles/flue.html — referring to Maria-Louise von Franz: *Die Visionen des Niklaus von Flüe*, Einsiedelin, Switzerland: Daimon, 1980.
167. Franz Kafka: July 21, 1913, *Kafka Diaries 1910–1913*, p. 292ff. Quoted in *I am a Memory Come Alive*, p. 89.
168. David J. Wallin: *Attachment in Psychotherapy*, p. 65.
169. Jean-Jacques Rousseau: *The Confessions*, p. 507.
170. Jean-Jacques Rousseau: *The Confessions*, p. 450.
171. Anthony Storr: *Solitude*, p. 95.
172. Anthony Storr: *Solitude*, p. xiii.
173. Laura Spinney: 'Why we do what we do', *New Scientist* magazine, July 31, 2004.
174. Martin Buber: *I and Thou*, p. 114, conversation between Indra and Prajapati.
175. Jean-Jacques Rousseau: *Émile*, p. 174.
176. Ralph Waldo Emerson: 'Self-reliance', *Selected Essays*, p. 193.
177. Jean-Jacques Rousseau: *The Reveries of the Solitary Walker*, p. 12.
178. Leonardo da Vinci: *The Notebooks of Leonardo da Vinci I*, translated by Jean Paul Richter (1888), No. 1154. Online at: http://www.naturalthinker.net/ trl/texts/Da%20Vinci,%20Leonardo/Da%20Vinci,% 20Leonardo%20-%20The%20Notebooks%20of.pdf
179. St. John Cassian: *The Training of a Monk and the Eight Deadly Sins*, Book X, Chapter 1. Online at: http://www.thenazareneway.com/Institutes%20of%2 0John%20Cassian/book_10_the%20_spirit_of_accidie. htm

180. W. B. Yeats: *The Yeats Reader: A Portable Compendium of Poetry, Drama, and Prose* (2002), p. 305. Quoted by Linda Spore online at: http://writing.colostate.edu/gallery/phantasmagoria/spore.htm
181. Walt Whitman: *Leaves of Grass*, lls 504/5.
182. Sylvia Plath: *The Unabridged Journals of Sylvia Plath*, No. 92, p. 76.
183. Toni Morrison: *A Mercy*, p. 46.
184. Friedrich Nietzsche: *Human all Too Human*, No. 559, p. 244.
185. Persius: *Satires*, I xxvi. English version by Máighréad Medbh. Latin text online at: http://archive.org/details/satiresofpersius00pers
186. Adam Phillips: *Promises, Promises*, p. 373–374.
187. Ralph Waldo Emerson: 'Self-reliance', *Selected Essays*, p. 175.
188. Ralph Waldo Emerson: 'Idealism', *Selected Essays*, p. 62.
189. Johann Wolfgang von Goethe: 'Erlkönig' / 'Erlking'. English version by Máighréad Medbh. German text online at: http://german.about.com/library/blerlking.htm
190. Michael S. Gazzaniga: 'The Split Brain Revisited', article in *The Hidden Mind, Scientific American Special Edition*, 2002.
191. Peter Høeg: 'Reflection of a Young Man in Balance', *Tales of The Night*, p. 305.
192. Henry David Thoreau: *Walden* (Conclusion), *Walden and Civil Disobedience,* p. 372.
193. Temple Grandin: *Thinking in Pictures*, p. 172.
194. Walt Whitman: *Leaves of Grass*, lls 1274–1275.
195. Thomas Gray: 'Elegy written in a Country Churchyard'. Online at: http://www.blupete.com/Literature/Poetry/Elegy.htm
196. Henry David Thoreau: *Walden* (Conclusion), *Walden and Civil Disobedience,* p. 369.
197. Barry Bonds of the San Francisco Giants: *USA Today*, July 3, 2001. Quoted in Anneli Rufus: *A Party of One*, p. 39.

198. Aldous Huxley: Introduction to *Bhagavad-Gita* (2002).
199. Martin Buber: *I and Thou*, p. 30.
200. Dylan Thomas: 'Light Breaks Where No Sun Shines', *Collected Poems 1934–1952*, p. 21.
201. George Santayana: *My Host the World*, p. 112.
202. Franz Kafka: June 16, 1913, *Franz Kafka, Letters to Felice* (1973), p. 269ff. Quoted in Nahum N. Glatzer, ed., *I am a Memory Come Alive*, p. 85.

BIBLIOGRAPHY

Agamben, Giorgio, *Stanzas*, Minneapolis: University of Minnesota Press, 1993.

Auden, W. H., *Collected Poems,* ed. Edward Mendelson, London: Faber and Faber, 1994.

Aurelius, Marcus, *Meditations (originally written 170–180 CE)*, New York: Dover, 1997.

———, *Meditations,* translated with an Introduction by Maxwell Staniforth, London: Penguin, 2004.

Baars, Bernard J. and Gage, Nicole M. eds., *Cognition, Brain and Consciousness*, London (UK), Burlington (MA), San Diego, (CA): Academic Press / Elsevier, 2010.

Bachelard, Gaston, *The Poetics of Space*, Boston: Beacon Press, 1994.

Badiou, Alain, *Being and Event,* London: Continuum, 2005.

Bhagavad-Gita: The Song of God, translated by Swami Prabhavanda and Christopher Isherwood, Introduction by Aldous Huxley, New York: Signet Classics (Penguin), 2002.

Birren, Faber, *Colour & Human Response*, Sussex: John Wiley & Sons Ltd, 1984.

Bishop, Elizabeth, *Complete Poems*, London: Chatto & Windus, 1997.

Blake, William, *Selected Poems*, ed. P. H. Butler, London: J. M. Dent & Sons Ltd (Everyman's Library), 1988.

Borges, Jorge Luis, *The Total Library: Non-Fiction 1922–1986*, ed. Eliot Weinberger, translated by Esther Allen, Suzanne Jill Levine and Eliot Weinberger, London: Penguin, 2001.

———, *Labyrinths*, eds. Donald A. Yates and James E. Irby, London: Penguin, 2000.

Brontë, Emily / The Brontë Sisters, *Selected Poems*, ed. Stevie Davies, Manchester: Carcanet, 2002.

Buber, Martin, *I and Thou*, translated by Ronald Gregor Smith, Edinburgh: T. & T. Clark, 2002 (first edition 1937).

Cacioppo, John and Patrick, William, *Loneliness,* New York: W. W. Norton & Co., 2009.

Cage, John, *Silence: 50th Anniversary Edition*, Middletown, CT: Wesleyan University Press, 2011.

Camus, Albert, *The Plague*, translated by Stuart Gilbert, London: Penguin Modern Classics, 1973 (*La Peste* first published 1947, by Gallimard).

———, *The Outsider*, London: Penguin, 2000.

———, *The Myth of Sisyphus*, London: Hamish Hamilton Ltd, 1979.

Carson, Ciaran, *Collected Poems*, Oldcastle: The Gallery Press, 2008.

Chedid, Andrée, *Selected Poems of Andrée Chedid* (*Studies in French Literature*, Volume 21), edited and translated by Judy Pfau Cochran, Lewiston / Queenston / Lampeter: The Edwin Mellen Press, 1995.

Coetzee, J. M., *In the Heart of the Country*, London: Vintage, 2004.

Cousteau, Jacques, *The Silent World*, Washington, D.C.: National Geographic Books, 2004.

Dawkins, Richard, *The Selfish Gene*, Oxford: Oxford University Press, 2006.

———, *The Extended Phenotype*, Oxford: Oxford University Press, 1999.

Defoe, Daniel, *Robinson Crusoe*, London: Penguin, 2001 (originally published London: W. Taylor, 1719).

Dennett, Daniel C., *Consciousness Explained*, London: Penguin, 1993.

Descartes, René, *Discourse on Method and the Meditations*, London: Penguin Classics, 1971 (first published 1641).

Dickinson, Emily, *The Complete Poems of Emily Dickinson*, ed. Thomas H. Johnson, New York: Little, Brown and Co., 1961.

Dorje, Gyurme, translator, *Tibetan Book of the Dead*, eds. Graham Coleman and Thupten Jinpa, London: Penguin, 2005.

Duncan, David Ewing, *The Calendar*, London: Fourth Estate, 1999.

Emerson, Ralph Waldo, *Selected Essays*, Introduction by Larzer Ziff, London: Penguin Classics, 1985 (originally published 1841).

———, *Selected Prose and Poetry*, New York: Holt, Rinehart and Winston, 1969.

Franzen, Jonathan, *How to be Alone*, London: Fourth Estate, 2003.

Freud, Sigmund, *Civilization and its Discontents*, Introduction by Leo Barsani, translated by David McLintock, London: Penguin, 2002.

Geary, James, *We Are What We Think*, London: John Murray, 2005.

Grandin, Temple, *Emergence: Labeled Autistic*, New York: Warner Books, 1996.

———, *Thinking in Pictures*, New York: Vintage Books, 1996.

———, *Animals in Translation*, London: Bloomsbury, 2006.

Hanh, Thich Nhat, *The Heart of the Buddha's Teaching*, London: Random House (Rider), 2002.

———, *Present Moment, Wonderful Moment*, London: Random House (Rider), 2002.

Hart, Josephine, *Catching Life by the Throat*, London: Virago, 2006.

Hartnett, Michael, *A Necklace of Wrens*, Oldcastle: Gallery Press, 2000.

———, *Collected Poems*, Oldcastle: Gallery Press, 2001.

———, *Translations*, Oldcastle: Gallery Press, 2003.

———, *Collected Poems, Volume 1*, Dublin / Manchester: Raven Arts Press / Carcanet Press, 1984 / 1985.

Hesiod, *Works and Days*, translated by Hugh G. Evelyn-White, 1914. Online at: http://www.sacred-texts.com/cla/hesiod/works.htm

Høeg, Peter, *Tales of The Night*, translated by Barbara Haveland, London: Harvill, 1997.

Hoffer, Eric, *Reflections on the Human Condition*, Titusville: Hopewell Publications, 2006.

———, *The True Believer: Thoughts on the Nature of Mass Movements,* New York: HarperCollins, 2002 (originally published by Harper & Row, 1951).

Hofstadter, Douglas, *I am a Strange Loop*, New York: Basic Books, 2007.

Holden, Robert, *Happiness Now*, London: Hodder & Stoughton, 1998.

Hollingdale, R.J., *A Nietzsche Reader*, London: Penguin, 1977.

Houellebecq, Michel, *Atomised,* London: Heinemann, 2000.

——, *Platform,* New York: Vintage, 2004.

——, *The Possibility of an Island*, London: Weidenfeld and Nicholson, 2005.

——, *H.P. Lovecraft Against the World, Against Life,* London: Weidenfeld & Nicholson, 2005.

Humphreys, Christmas, *Zen: a Way of Life,* Maidenhead: McGraw-Hill, 1992.

Jung, Carl Gustav, *The Undiscovered Self,* Abingdon: Routledge & Kegan Paul, 2006.

Kafka, Franz, *I am a Memory Come Alive: Autobiographical Writings by Franz Kafka*, ed. Nahum N. Glatzer, N. Y.: Schocken Books, 1974.

——, *Franz Kafka: Letters to Felice*, eds. Erich Heller and Jürgen Born, translated by James Stern and Elisabeth Duckworth, N. Y.: Schocken Books, 1973.

——, *Letters to Felice*, eds. Erich Heller and Jürgen Born, translated by James Stern and Elisabeth Duckworth, London: Martin Secker & Warburg Ltd, 1974.

——, *Kafka Diaries 1910–1913*, ed. Max Brod, translated by Joseph Kresh, New York: Schocken Books, 1948.

Keats, John: *Letters of John Keats, Vol. 1*, ed. H. E. Rollins, Cambridge: Harvard University Press, 1958.

Keenan, Brian, *An Evil Cradling*, London: Vintage, 1993.

Kierkegaard, Søren, *The Essential Kierkegaard*, eds. Howard V. Hong and Edna H. Hong, Princeton: Princeton University Press, 2000.

Kundera, Milan, *Immortality*, translated by P. Kussi, London: Faber and Faber, 1992.

——, *Book of Laughter and Forgetting,* translated from the French by Aaron Asher, London: Faber and Faber, 2000.

Larkin, Philip, *Collected Poems*, ed. Anthony Twaite, London: Faber and Faber, 1990, 2003.

Levi, Primo, *The Periodic Table*, translated by Raymond Rosenthal, London: David Campbell Publishers Ltd (Everyman's Library), 1995.

Levin, Bernard, *Enthusiasms*, London: Jonathan Cape, 1983.

Mackenzie, Vicki, *Cave in the Snow*, London: Bloomsbury, 1998.

McEwan, Ian, *Saturday*, London: Jonathan Cape, 2005.

MacNeice, Louis, *Collected Poems*, London: Faber and Faber, 2007.

Maddocks, Fiona, *Hildegard of Bingen*, London: Hodder Headline, 2001.

Maitland, Sara, *A Book of Silence*, London: Granta Books, 2008.

Mannin, Ethel, *Loneliness*, London: Hutchinson & Co. Ltd, 1966.

Margulis, Lynn and Sagan, Dorion, *What is Life?*, London: Weidenfeld & Nicolson, 1995.

Matthews, Eric, *Mind: Key Concepts in Philosophy Series*, London: Continuum, 2005.

Merton, Thomas, *The Seven Storey Mountain*, London: Sheldon Press, 1975.

Milton, John, *Paradise Lost*, Oxford and New York: Oxford University Press, 2008.

Montaigne, Michel de, *The Complete Essays*, translated by M. A. Screech, London: Penguin, 1991.

———, *Les Essais, Livre 1*, l'édition Millanges de 1580. Online at: http://www.lib.uchicago.edu/efts/ARTFL/projects/montaigne/1580essais1.html

Moore, Thomas, *The Care of the Soul*, London: Piatkus Books, 1992.

Morrison, Toni, *A Mercy*, London: Chatto & Windus, 2008.

Nabokov, Vladimir, *The Luzhin Defense*, translated by Michael Scammell, London: Penguin, 2000.

Newton, Michael, *Savage Girls and Wild Boys*, London: Faber and Faber, 2002.

Nietzsche, Friedrich, *Thus Spake Zarathustra*, translated by R. J. Hollingdale, London: Penguin, 1984.

———, *Human, All Too Human*, translated by Marion Faber and Stephen Lehmann, Introduction by Marion Faber, London: Penguin, 2004.

————, *The Birth of Tragedy*, translated by Clifton Fadiman, Mineola, New York: Dover Publications, 1995.

Noakes, Tim, *The Lore of Running*, Illinois: Human Kinetics, 2001.

Phillips, Adam, *Promises, Promises*, London: Faber and Faber, 2000.

Plath, Sylvia, *The Unabridged Journals of Sylvia Plath*, ed. Karen V. Kukil, New York: Anchor Books / Random House, 2000.

Prince-Hughes, Dawn, *Songs of the Gorilla Nation*, New York: Three Rivers Press, 2005.

Purkiss, Diane, *Troublesome Things*, London: Penguin, 2000.

Rich, Adrienne, *The Dream of a Common Language: Poems 1974-1977*, New York / London: W. W. Norton & Co., 1993.

Ridley, Matt, *The Origins of Virtue*, London: Penguin, 1997.

Rilke, Rainer Maria, *Letters to a Young Poet*, translated by M. D. Herter Norton, N. Y.: W. W. Norton & Co., 2004.

————, *The Essential Rilke*, selected and translated by Galway Kinnell and Hannah Liebmann, New Jersey: Ecco Press, 1999.

————, *Uncollected Poems*, translated by Edward Snow, New York: Farrar, Straus and Giroux, 1997.

Rollins, H. E. ed., *Letters of John Keats Vol. 1*, Cambridge: Harvard University Press, 1958.

Rousseau, Jean-Jacques, *The Confessions*, translated by J. M. Cohen, London: Everyman's Library, 1992 (first published 1782).

————, *Émile*, translated by Barbara Foxley, London: Everyman's Library, 1974 (first published 1762).

————, *The Social Contract and the Discourses*, translated by G. D. H. Cole, London: Everyman's Library, 1993 (first published 1762).

————, *The Reveries of the Solitary Walker*, translated by Charles E. Butterworth, Indianapolis: Hackett Publishing Company, 1992 (first published 1782).

————, *The Discourses and Other Early Political Writings*, translated and edited by Victor Gourevitch, Cambridge: Cambridge University Press, 1997.

Rufus, Anneli, *Party of One: The Loner's Manifesto*, New York: Marlowe & Company, 2003.

Sacks, Oliver, *The Man who Mistook his Wife for a Hat*, New York: Touchstone, 1998.

Santayana, George, *My Host the World*, London: The Cresset Press, 1953.

Sartre, Jean-Paul, *Being and Nothingness*, translated by Hazel E. Barnes, London: Routledge, 1972.

Schopenhauer, Arthur, *The World as Will and Idea*, ed. David Berman, translated by Jill Berman, London: J. M. Dent & Sons, 1995.

Scientific American Special Edition: The Hidden Mind, 2002. http://www.scientificamerican.com/special/toc.cfm?issue id=11

Stoltzfus, Ben, *Lacan and Literature: Purloined Texts*, N. Y.: the State University of New York Press, 1996.

Storr, Anthony, *Solitude*, London: HarperCollins, 1997.

———, *The Integrity of the Personality*, London: Heinemann Medical, 1960; Pelican Books, 1977.

Tammett, Daniel, *Born on a Blue Day*, London: Hodder & Stoughton, 2006.

Thomas, Dylan, *Collected Poems 1934–1952*, London: J. M. Dent & Sons, 1984.

Thoreau, Henry David, *Walden and Civil Disobedience*, London: Penguin Classics, 1986.

Truss, Lynne, *Talk to the Hand*, London: Profile, 2007.

Tyndall, John, *Address delivered before the British Association at Belfast*, London: Longman, Green & Co., 1874. Online at: http://www.victorianweb.org/science/science_texts/ belfast.html

Vitebsky, Piers, *The Shaman*, London: Duncan Baird, 2001.

Wallin, David J., *Attachment in Psychotherapy*, London: Guilford Press, 2007.

Waugh, Alexander, *Time*, London: Headline, 2000.

Weber, Ann L., *Introduction to Psychology*, New York: HarperCollins, 1991.

White, Emily, *Lonely*, New York: HarperCollins, 2010.

Whitman, Walt, *Leaves of Grass, The First (1855) edition*, ed. Malcolm Crowley, London: Penguin Classics, 1986.

Wilde, Oscar, *The Picture of Dorian Gray*, London: Penguin, 2003.

——, *The Picture of Dorian Gray*, Oxford: Oxford University Press, 2008.

Wilson, Rick, *The Man Who Was Robinson Crusoe*, Glasgow: Neil Wilson Publishing Ltd, 2009.

Wing, Laura, *The Autistic Spectrum*, London: Constable, 2003.

Wittkower, Margot and Rudolph, *Born Under Saturn*, New York: New York Review of Books (NYRB), 2007.

Woolf, Virginia, *A Room of One's Own*, London: Hogarth Press, 1978.

Wurtzel, Elizabeth, *Prozac Nation: Young and Depressed in America – A Memoir*, London: Quartet Books, 1996.

Yeats, W. B., *Collected Poems*, London: Macmillan, 1985.

——, *The Yeats Reader: A Portable Compendium of Poetry, Drama, and Prose*, ed. Richard J. Finneran, New York: Scribner Poetry, 2002.

Zohar, Danah: *The Quantum Self*, New York: Quill, 1990.

ACKNOWLEDGEMENTS

Excerpt from unpublished thesis, *The Development of Autobiography in Western Culture: from Augustine to Rousseau*, by Peter Abbs, quoted by permission of the author.

Excerpt from 'The Riddle', Copyright © 1940 by W. H. Auden, renewed, from *Collected Poems of W. H. Auden*. Used by permission of Random House, Inc. and Curtis Brown, Ltd.

Excerpts from *Meditations* by Marcus Aurelius, Copyright © Maxwell Staniforth, 1964, reprinted by permission of Penguin UK.

Excerpt from *Cognition, Brain and Consciousness*, by Bernard J. Baars and Nicole M. Gage, London (UK), Burlington (MA), San Diego (CA): Academic Press / Elsevier, 2010, reprinted by permission of Elsevier.

Excerpt from Leo Barsani, Introduction to Sigmund Freud, *Civilization and its Discontents,* reprinted by permission of Penguin UK. Translation copyright © David McLintock, 2002.

Excerpt from 'In the Waiting Room' from *The Complete Poems 1927–1979* by Elizabeth Bishop, Copyright © 1979, 1983 by Alice Helen Methfessel, reprinted by permission of Farrar, Straus and Giroux, LLC.

Excerpt from *Loneliness* by John Cacioppo and William Patrick, 2009, reprinted by permission of W. W. Norton & Company Inc.

Excerpt from *Silence: 50th Anniversary Edition,* © 2011 by John Cage, reprinted by permission of Wesleyan University Press.

Selections from *Collected Poems* by Ciaran Carson, 2008, reprinted by kind permission of Gallery Press, Oldcastle, Co. Meath.

Excerpt from 'Landscapes' / 'Paysages' by Andrée Chedid reprinted by permission of Judy Pfau Cochran, translator, 1995.

Excerpt from *H.P. Lovecraft Against the World, Against Life* by Michel Houellebecq, 2005, reprinted by permission of Orion Publishing Group and Éditions du Rocher.

Excerpt from Aldous Huxley, Introduction to *Bhagavad-Gita: The Song of God*, 2002, reprinted by permission of Vedanta Press, Hollywood, CA.

Excerpts from *The Undiscovered Self* by Carl Gustav Jung, 2006, reprinted by permission of Routledge / Taylor & Francis Group, UK.

Excerpt from *Letters to Felice* by Franz Kafka, published by Secker & Warburg, 1974, reprinted by permission of The Random House Group Limited.

Excerpts from *The Essential Kierkegaard,* eds. Howard V. Hong and Edna H. Hong, 2000, reprinted by permission of Princeton University Press.

Excerpt from *Immortality* by Milan Kundera, translated by P. Kussi, 1992, reprinted by permission of Faber and Faber.

Selections from Philip Larkin's *Collected Poems,* 1990, 2003, reprinted by permission of Faber and Faber.

Excerpt from *Saturday* by Ian McEwan, published by Jonathan Cape, 2005, reprinted by permission of The Random House Group Limited.

Selections from *Collected Poems* by Louis MacNeice, published by Faber and Faber, quoted by permission of David Higham Associates.

Excerpt from *Cave in the Snow* © Vicki Mackenzie, 1998, reprinted by permission of Bloomsbury Publishing Plc.

Excerpts from *A Book of Silence* by Sara Maitland, 2008, reprinted by permission of Granta Books.

Excerpts from *The Seven Storey Mountain* by Thomas Merton, London: Sheldon Press, 1975, reprinted by permission of SPCK Publishing.

Maria Montessori quotation by permission of Montessori Scotts Valley.

Excerpt from *Care of the Soul* by Thomas Moore, 1992, reprinted by permission of Little, Brown Book Group.

Lightning Source UK Ltd.
Milton Keynes UK
UKOW05f1042120813

215232UK00001B/5/P